cold tangerines

It would be good for all of us if Shauna Niequist would promise to write a book like *Cold Tangerines* every year or two for the rest of our lives. Her sensitivity would sensitize us. Her honesty would puncture our pretentions. Her spiritual insight would take us deeper. Her beautiful literary style would ignite our imaginations. And her love—for life, for family, for God—would recenter us on what matters most. Let's hope this is the first of many books from this talented, new first-rate writer.

Brian McLaren, author and speaker

I could not put down this remarkable book. But after the last page, I wanted to hug my kids harder, *really* taste the raspberries at dinner, and do a happy dance for the stunning gift of life. Shauna uses words to tap into the raw emotions of our humanity—joy, deep sadness, surprise, anger, jealousy, and most of all, delight. Not only do her stories open up a window into the life of this young woman, they also tap into all of our stories, reminding us of the wonder and privilege it is to walk for a time on this planet.

Nancy Beach, author and teaching pastor at Willow Creek Community Church

cold tangerines

celebrating the extraordinary nature of everyday life

shauna niequist

ZONDERVAN®

ZONDERVAN.com/
AUTHORTRACKER
follow your favorite authors

ZONDERVAN®

Cold Tangerines
Copyright © 2007 by Shauna Niequist

This title is also available in a Zondervan audio edition.
Visit www.zondervan.fm.

Requests for information should be addressed to:
Zondervan, *Grand Rapids, Michigan* 49530

Library of Congress Cataloging-in-Publication Data

Niequist, Shauna.
    Cold tangerines : celebrating the extraordinary nature of everyday life /
Shauna Niequist.
      p.   cm.
    ISBN 978-0-310-27360-8
    1. Christian life. I. Title.
  BV4515.3.N54   2007
  242—dc22

                  2007026417

Internet addresses (websites, blogs, etc.) and telephone numbers printed in this book
are offered as a resource to you. These are not intended in any way to be or imply an
endorsement on the part of Zondervan, nor do we vouch for the content of these sites
and numbers for the life of this book.

Published in association with Yates & Yates, LLP, Attorneys and Counselors, Orange,
California.

Printed in the United States of America

08 09 10 11 12 13 • 22 21 20 19 18 17 16 15 14 13 12 11 10 9 8 7 6 5

For Bill, Lynne, and Todd

It is a profound miracle when
family bonds weave beyond themselves
and bind us into true friendship.

For Annette, Andrew, and Spence Richards,
Steve and Sarah Carter, and Joe Hays

It is another kind of miracle entirely
when friendship bends beyond itself
and binds us into family.

And most of all, for Aaron and Henry

For sharing with me the daily glittering miracles
of marriage, motherhood,
and love.

contents

III

IV

introduction

This book is a shameless appeal for celebration.

I know that the world is several versions of mad right now. I know that pessimism and grimness sometimes seem like the only responsible choices. I wake up at night and think about pesticides and international politics and fundamentalism and disease and roadside bombs and the fact that one day my parents will die. I had a hard year this year, the hardest I've yet known. I worry about the world we're creating for my baby boy. I get the pessimism and the grimness.

And that's why I'm making a shameless appeal for celebration. Because I need to. I need optimism and celebration and hope in the face of violence and despair and anxiety. And because the other road is a dead end. Despair is a slow death, and a lifetime of anger is like a lifetime of hard drinking: it shows in your face and your eyes and your words even when you think it doesn't.

The only option, as I see it, is this delicate weaving of action and celebration, of intention and expectation. Let's act, read, protest, protect, picket, learn, advocate for, fight against, but let's be careful that in the midst of all that accomplishing and organizing, we don't bulldoze over a world that's teeming with beauty and hope and redemption all around us and in the meantime. Before the wars are over, before the cures are found, before the wrongs are righted, Today, humble Today, presents itself to us with all the ceremony and bling of a glittering diamond ring: *Wear me, it says. Wear me out. Love me, dive into me, discover me*, it pleads with us.

The discipline of celebration is changing my life, and it is because of the profound discoveries that this way of living affords to me that I invite you into the same practice. This collection is a tap dance on the fresh graves of apathy and cynicism, the creeping belief that this is all there is, and that God is no match for the wreckage of the world we live in. What God does in the tiny corners of our day-to-day lives is stunning and gorgeous and headline-making, but we have a bad habit of saving the headlines for the grotesque and scary.

There are a lot of good books about what's wrong, what's broken, what needs fixing and dismantling and deconstructing. They're good books. I read them, and I hope you do, too. But there might be a little voice inside of you, like there is inside of me, a voice that asks, "Is that all? Is this all there is?" And to that tiny, holy voice, I say, "No way, kiddo, there's so much more, and it's all around us, and it's right in front of our eyes."

To choose to celebrate in the world we live in right now might seem irresponsible. It might seem frivolous, like cotton candy and charm bracelets. But I believe it is a serious undertaking, and one that has the potential to return us to our best selves, to deliver us back to the men and women God created us to be, people who choose to see the best, believe the best, yearn for the best. Through that longing to be our best selves, we are changed and inspired and ennobled, able to see the handwriting of a holy God where another person just sees the same old tired streets and sidewalks.

These are my stories, the stories of life as it reveals itself in my field of vision, and the cast of characters are my friends and family and neighbors. I'm telling these stories because they're the only ones I know and the only ones I have the right to tell, believing that in them you will find your own stories, with your own beautiful and strange characters and plot twists. I believe that these love letters to my own quotidian life might possibly unmask the tiny glimmers of hope and redemption masquerading as normal life in your corner of the world.

The world is alive, blinking and clicking, winking at us slyly, inviting us to get up and dance to the music that's been playing since the beginning of time, if you bend all the way down and put your ear to the ground to listen for it.

I

on waiting

I have always, essentially, been waiting. Waiting to become something else, waiting to be that person I always thought I was on the verge of becoming, waiting for that life I thought I would have. In my head, I was always one step away. In high school, I was biding my time until I could become the college version of myself, the one my mind could see so clearly. In college, the post-college "adult" person was always looming in front of me, smarter, stronger, more organized. Then the married person, then the person I'd become when we have kids. For twenty years, literally, I have waited to become the thin version of myself, because that's when life will really begin.

And through all that waiting, here I am. My life is passing, day by day, and I am waiting for it to start. I am waiting for that time, that person, that event when my life will finally begin.

I love movies about "The Big Moment"—the game or the performance or the wedding day or the record deal, the stories that split time with that key event, and everything is reframed, before it and after it, because it has changed everything. I have always wanted this movie-worthy event, something that will change everything and grab me out of this waiting game into the whirlwind in front of me. I cry and cry at these movies, because I am still waiting for my own big moment. I had visions of life as an adventure, a thing to be celebrated and experienced, but all I was doing was going to work and coming home, and that wasn't what it looked like in the movies.

John Lennon once said, "Life is what happens when you're busy making other plans." For me, life is what was happening while I was busy waiting for my big moment. I was ready for it and believed that the rest of my life would fade into the background, and that my big moment would carry me through life like a lifeboat.

The Big Moment, unfortunately, is an urban myth. Some people have them, in a sense, when they win the Heisman or become the next American Idol. But even that football player or that singer is living a life made up of more than that one moment. Life is a collection of a million, billion moments, tiny little moments and choices, like a handful of luminous, glowing pearls. And strung together, built upon one another, lined up through the days and the years, they make a life, a person. It takes so much time, and so much work, and those beads and moments are so small, and so much less fabulous and dramatic than the movies.

But this is what I'm finding, in glimpses and flashes: this is it. This is it, in the best possible way. That thing I'm waiting for, that adventure, that movie-score-worthy experience unfolding gracefully. This is it. Normal, daily life ticking by on our streets and sidewalks, in our houses and apartments, in our beds and at our dinner tables, in our dreams and prayers and fights and secrets—this pedestrian life is the most precious thing any of us will ever experience.

I believe that this way of living, this focus on the present, the daily, the tangible, this intense concentration not on the news headlines but on the flowers growing in your own garden, the children growing in your own home, this way of living has the potential to open up the heavens, to yield a glittering handful of diamonds where a second ago there was coal. This way of living and noticing and building and crafting can crack through the movie sets and soundtracks that keep us waiting for our own life stories to begin, and set us free to observe the lives we have been creating all along without even realizing it.

I don't want to wait anymore. I choose to believe that there is nothing more sacred or profound than this day. I choose to believe that there may be a thousand big moments embedded in this day, waiting to be discovered like tiny shards of gold. The big moments are the daily, tiny moments of courage and forgiveness and hope that we grab on to and extend to one another. That's the drama of life, swirling all around us, and generally I don't even see it, because I'm too busy waiting to become whatever it is I think I am about to become. The big moments are in every hour, every conversation, every meal, every meeting.

The Heisman Trophy winner knows this. He knows that his big moment was not when they gave him the trophy. It was the thousand times he went to practice instead of going back to bed. It was the miles run on rainy days, the healthy meals when a burger sounded like heaven. That big moment represented and rested on a foundation of moments that had come before it.

I believe that if we cultivate a true attention, a deep ability to see what has been there all along, we will find worlds within us and between us, dreams and stories and memories spilling over. The nuances and shades and secrets and intimations of love and friendship and marriage and parenting are action-packed and multicolored, if you know where to look.

Today is your big moment. Moments, really. The life you've been waiting for is happening all around you. The scene unfolding right outside your window is worth more than the most beautiful painting, and the crackers and peanut butter that you're having for lunch on the coffee table are as profound, in their own way, as the Last Supper. This is it. This is life in all its glory, swirling and unfolding around us, disguised as pedantic, pedestrian non-events. But pull off the mask and you will find your life, waiting to be made, chosen, woven, crafted.

Your life, right now, today, is exploding with energy and power and detail and dimension, better than the best movie you have ever seen. You and your family and your friends and your house and your dinner table and your garage have all the makings of a life of epic proportions, a story for the ages. Because they all are. Every life is.

You have stories worth telling, memories worth remembering, dreams worth working toward, a body worth feeding, a soul worth tending, and beyond that, the God of the universe dwells within you, the true culmination of super and natural.

You are more than dust and bones.

You are spirit and power and image of God.

And you have been given Today.

spark

I loved going to church when I was little. Our church used to meet in a movie theater, and my Sunday school class was right by the candy counter, so it always smelled like popcorn, and we would press our faces up against the glass of the counter, looking at all the bright shiny candy boxes. It felt glamorous and exciting and busy, and there was something exhilarating and illicit about being in a movie theater when they weren't showing movies, like you were at an after-hours party. While I was in Sunday school, my parents were in Big Church. My dad gave the message and sang in the band, and my mom played the flute. When church was over, I'd run down the sloped theater aisle to find them on the stage, and I was very fast, especially because of the sloped floor.

I loved going to church until about halfway through high school, when I got tired of being a church girl, of being one of the only church girls in my group of friends at school, the only one on my pom squad, the only one at the party who never had to worry about taking a Breathalyzer. When I played powder-puff football, I missed the day we chose nicknames for our jerseys, and my friends chose mine for me. All their names were thinly veiled drinking references or allusions to scandalous dating experiences. When I picked up my jersey, it said, "Church Lady."

I knew they loved me and that they knew I was more than a *Saturday Night Live* sketch, but it hurt me. I didn't want to be that person anymore. I was tired of being different, and underneath that, I wanted to know why it was worth being so different. I was different because that's the way I had grown up, and I needed to see if it was what I would have chosen on my own. I was starting to think that being a Christian, for me, was like being Italian or being short—something you're born into, that's out of your control, but something that will define your life. I wanted to see what I could do with my life on my own terms.

I went to Westmont College in Santa Barbara, two thousand miles from my town and my high school near Chicago. My decision to go there was partially out of heartbreak and desperation, having been rejected from my dream school, and partially out of a strange, deep feeling in my stomach that almost felt like hunger, a feeling I believe was God's urging. The great thing about a Christian college is that if you have some good old-fashioned rebelling to do, it's not that hard to be bad because there are so many rules. I had a tiny tattoo that I got in high school, and I got another one in Santa Barbara, a thin vine winding around my toe. I skipped chapel and pierced my nose and lived off campus and smoked cigarettes, and that's about all it took to be a bad girl. Another truly great thing about a college like Westmont is that there are lots of really good people, professors and fellow students alike, who will catch you when you fall down, and I fell down a lot.

During that season, all I could see about faith were the things that offended me, the things I couldn't connect with, the things that had embarrassed me in front of my friends. But even then, there was this tiny hope inside me, not like a flame, more like a lighter that's almost out of juice, misfiring, catching for just a second, this tiny hope that maybe there was a way of living this faith that I just hadn't found yet.

I thought about God, even though I didn't talk about him. It wasn't really about God, for me. I didn't have big questions on the nature of the Trinity or the end of the world. Essentially, I wanted to know if there was room in the Christian world for someone like me. Because it didn't always seem like there was.

The journey back toward faith came in flashes and moments and entirely through pain. I wanted to build my life on my own terms. I felt like having faith was like having training wheels on your bike, and I wanted to ride without those training wheels even if I fell. For a while, I loved it. I felt creative and smart and courageous.

And then everything unraveled over the course of a year. I had three best friends, and two of them went to Europe, and I fell in love with the third one, or more accurately, admitted to him that I'd loved him for years. I thought we'd get married. We talked about it, and we made plans, and we dreamed about our future. And then one day it was over. We screamed at each other in the driveway of my house in Montecito, my roommates trying unsuccessfully not to eavesdrop. He was, in his words, simply not ready for such a serious relationship. Oddly enough, soon after we broke up, he was ready for a very serious relationship with one of my friends. Ah.

I was heartbroken and confused and very much alone, and I started doing the craziest things. If you're a really sensible, stable person, and somebody breaks your heart, you might do something wild, like go out dancing and drinking all night, but that's what I did on normal days.

I dug out my Bible. I have no idea why, really. I sat alone on my bed on a Saturday afternoon with the light slanting through my window. I was a literature major, so my room was crammed with books, and underneath a tall stack of books on the windowsill, I found my Bible. I just held it. I don't think I even read it that day. I just held it on my lap with both hands, like it was a cat.

I joined a Bible study with some fine upstanding girls from my college. I'm sure they wondered what on earth I was doing there. I was wondering the same thing.

There was something inside me that was pushing me toward God, pushing me toward the church. And it was like learning to walk after an accident—my body recalling so much, feeling so familiar, but entirely new this time. I started going to church, but that didn't work right away, because when I went, I could still only hear the things that distanced me or the things that made me mad, the clichés and assumptions that had pushed me away in the first place.

I wanted to connect with God somehow, so I decided that I would go to the beach every night at sunset. It was the most sacred thing I could think to do. I wasn't ready yet for church, but I was ready for God, and I have always believed that the ocean is one of the surest places to find him. I sat on the wall at Biltmore Beach in Montecito and waited. I started praying a little bit more honestly and listening a little bit more closely. It was like seeing an old boyfriend, all shy and tentative, but really excited on the inside.

There was something inside me, some hopeful, small, faltering voice that said, "There's room for you." I don't know why, but I trusted that voice.

And against all odds, demonstrating that God is in fact very gracious and kind of a jokester, here I am, deeply, wholly committed to God and to his church. I tried as hard as I could to find a better way to live, to move past or through or beyond this tradition and set of ideas and practices that had defined my life. I separated myself from the language and the circles and the people who represented that world, and I couldn't wait to find that other thing, that better thing. And as I traveled and pushed and explored, I started realizing with a cringe that the road was leading me dangerously close to the start, and I was finding myself drawn against all odds, against my intentions, to this way of living, this way of Jesus, this way of passion and compassion that I had grown up in.

My parents, I think, were as surprised as I was. They watched me fall in love with several of the loveliest but most unsuitable boyfriends, watched me barrel down several of the most ridiculous paths, watched me learn from the same mistakes over and over and over until it seemed like maybe I wasn't learning at all.

There's a lot of pressure on pastors to coerce their kids into looking the part, or to distance themselves from kids whose mistakes reflect poorly on their churches. My parents did just the opposite: they flew across the country several times a year to be with me, to demonstrate to me that no matter how ferociously I fought for space in a world that felt like it had no room for me, they would be right there, right next to me, helping me fight and helping me make peace.

I loved those years. Those years made me believe in the journey and respect it, the way you respect deep water if you've ever swam out too far and been surprised by the waves. I know what that journey can do in people. I know what it did in me, and I don't take it lightly. I have some very sobering scars and memories that I carry with me as reminders of that season. They remind me how dangerous that path is, and how beautiful.

Along the way, I've collected more questions than answers, but I've fought for a few ideas that have formed a bed I can rest on, a life I can make peace with, a dream I can cling to. I'm not a doctrinarian, mostly because for me, doctrine is not the thing that God has used to change my life. I'm a reader and a storyteller, and God chose literature and story and poetry as the languages of my spiritual text. To me, the Bible is a manifesto, a guide, a love letter, a story. To me, life with God is prismatic, shocking, demanding, freeing. It's the deepest stream, the blood in my veins, the stories and words of my dreams and my middle-of-the-night prayers. I am still surprised on a regular basis at the love I feel for the spirit of God, the deep respect and emotion that I experience when I see an expanse of water or a new baby or the kindness of strangers.

I'm immeasurably thankful to have been born into a community of faith. And I'm even more thankful that my community of faith allowed me the space and freedom to travel my own distances around and through the questions I needed to answer. I'm thankful for the patience and grace I was given, for the forgiveness I was extended, and the guidance I needed.

I'm thankful for God's constant flickering and sparking flame inside me, planted in me years ago and fighting to keep burning. For a season, I didn't think it mattered much, but now I know that tiny flame is the most precious thing I have, and that it can ignite a forest fire inside any heart and can burn away a lifetime of apathy and regret and distance.

becoming family

Aaron and I were married five years ago, on a hot August night on Michigan Avenue in Chicago, near the lake and Buckingham Fountain and the Art Institute. I walked down the aisle to a Beatles song, and we danced and ate crab cakes and chocolate cake from Sweet Thang in Wicker Park, and lots of our friends sang along with the band. We watched the fireworks over Navy Pier blend in with the sizzle of the city sky. It was both sweet and a little bit wild, like the best parties are.

On that hot shimmering night, one of the things I said to Aaron in our wedding vows was, "When I am with you, wherever we are, I am home." It was, I thought, a beautiful and romantic thing to say, and I really felt it. Aaron has a way of settling me down and making peace in me when everything feels crazy and alien. The more time I spent with him when we first met, the stronger and more peaceful I felt, like I had eaten a delicious and nutritious breakfast.

I didn't actually think, though, that I would have to put our vows into practice quite so quickly. We met and dated in the town both our families lived in, and when we got married, we lived in that same town, near old friends and cousins and siblings. And then just a few months after our first anniversary, a friend of ours asked us to think about moving to be a part of his church, three hours away, for Aaron to be a worship leader there. It was in Grand Rapids, Michigan.

The only time we had been to Grand Rapids was for a Faith Hill and Tim McGraw concert with my parents. My dad is a country music fan, and Aaron was taking one for the team, country music fan that he is not. I developed a little bit of a crush on Tim McGraw when he sang the one about the barbecue stain on the white T-shirt, and even Aaron could appreciate the show, although I think he was mostly appreciating Faith Hill's legs.

We drove up to Grand Rapids to talk to our friend about the church, and when we got back into the car, I started to cry, and continued crying most of the way back to Chicago. Aaron, I could see, was very excited about the prospect of the move, and very puzzled by the tears. It was an honor that they would invite him into this job. And all I could do was cry. When he asked me, gently, why I was crying, the first thing that came out was, "I feel like I'm marching to my death." He was silent for a moment after that. I'm not sure that's exactly what he wanted me to say, and I'm not sure that's exactly what I meant. I think what I meant is that I could feel, right then, the inevitability of it, that I knew somehow that we were moving, and I had already begun to mourn. I don't think either of us knew then that I would mourn, in waves, for the first two years that we lived in Grand Rapids.

When I said to him on our wedding day that when I was with him, I was home, I did not mean, "Let's move to Michigan and see if I'm right, okay?" I meant, "I love you so much, and let's stay in Chicago where my parents and my friends are, how about that?" But I said, before God and seven bridesmaids, that Aaron is my home, my partner, my number one, and so now I live in Michigan. The moral of the story, I suppose, is that, if at all possible, you should make your wedding vows very noncommittal and easy to keep. Things like, "If you have an idea, I'll consider it, most of the time," or "If it doesn't interfere with my own plans, I'd be happy to hear your request." I, however, was quite naïve and promised to live, no matter what, with and for and deeply connected to this other person. Thank God.

I had thought that we became a family the day we were married. What I have found, though, is that the web starts as just one fine filament on that day, and spins and spins around us as life presents itself to us day by day. And on some days, the strands spin around us double-time, spinning us like a top and binding us like rubber cement.

September 11, 2001, was a Tuesday. Aaron and I had been married for two weeks and had arrived home two days before from our honeymoon to Sydney and the Great Barrier Reef. And I'm using the word *home* loosely. Aaron was moving into my little house, and I had not made any space for him or his things before the wedding. The floor of the loft was covered with wedding presents and ribbons and torn wrapping paper, and every available surface was littered with one or another wedding related item—leftover programs, clothes for the honeymoon that didn't make it into the bag and needed to be returned, favor ideas gone awry. All his earthly belongings were piled into the basement and the garage, and I remember secretly thinking that that wasn't a bad place for them, given the limited space in the house. The bathroom and the closet were of special concern, and he lived for a few days like a college student in a dorm, with his toothbrush and razor packed into his shaving kit, toting it in and out of the bathroom.

Immediately before the wedding, I had acted on an ill-conceived idea to use the tiny dining area as a sort of Roman reclining-and-dining area, with two enormous but extremely uncomfortable wicker-ish throne-like chairs, each with an ottoman. I guess I thought that rather than a little table for four wedged in between the kitchen and the living room, this would be a more interesting and less conventional use of space, and I liked the idea of us curled up on these palatial chairs, watching the news and talking about our days. They were so big that we had to turn sideways to get to the kitchen, and so uncomfortable that Aaron boycotted them almost immediately. The only reason I remember them, I think, is that on September 11, we sat on them and watched the news for hours. Later that week, the chairs went back to the store at Aaron's insistence.

I remember coming home from work that day and having the clear sense that that night, the evening of September 11, was one to be spent with family. At that time, and at our age then, we didn't totally understand the implications of what had happened. No one did, of course, but perhaps least of all us, who had grown up in an age of so little violence and war, at least to our awareness. We knew, though, instinctively, that that was a night to spend with family, and we realized with a jolt that that's what we were. We were family.

It's hard to imagine now, now that we have been married for five years, now that we live in another state, in our home, one with space for me and space for him. Now we are, certainly, family. Aaron is my first thought and last thought, the companion with whom I walk through every part of life.

But he wasn't yet, at that point. A wedding didn't make him my family, or a honeymoon, or grudgingly giving him one half of the storage space in the bathroom (let's be honest—

one quarter). What did make him my family, though, was the decision to stay home with him on that Tuesday night, to sit in those horribly uncomfortable chairs, holding hands across their massive, prickly arms, watching the news for hours. Our first impulse was to go home, to my parents' house and to his, and we stared at each other for a moment in the living room, wondering what to do. We stayed in a house that didn't particularly feel like home for either one of us at that point, and I think it became a little bit more of a home that night.

That's how family gets made. Not by ceremonies or certificates, and not by parties and celebrations. Family gets made when you decide to hold hands and sit shoulder to shoulder when it seems like the sky is falling. Family gets made when the world becomes strange and disorienting, and the only face you recognize is his. Family gets made when the future obscures itself like a solar eclipse, and in the intervening darkness, you decide that no matter what happens in the night, you'll face it as one.

And so, Aaron, thank you for becoming, and for being, my family. Thank you for persuading me to take back the chairs, and thank you for sitting with me that night, and thousands of nights since then, watching and listening to our world change, with two sets of eyes and ears instead of one. Thank you for the millions of ways you have been my family since then, but especially, thank you for being my family that night.

puppies

*for Ashley, Stacey, Rosey, Stef, Mer, Krystina,
Christel, Kristin, Katharine, and Jes*

I was so sad one night just after we moved to Grand
Rapids, and I was trying to find the words to tell Aaron how
I was feeling, and this was the only way I could describe it:
when I lived in Santa Barbara, my friends had a Jack Russell
terrier named Little, and when Little had puppies, I helped
take care of them. There were six of them in a cardboard box,
and they huddled together to keep each other warm, and
they didn't want to be held, even if you held them very tight,
because really they just wanted to be back in the box with
the other puppies. I told Aaron that I felt like someone took
me out of the box, and all I wanted was that feeling of being
right next to my puppy-friends. I told him that I felt like I was
freezing cold all the time, and all I wanted was to be back
with the rest of the little puppies who kept me warm.

Eight years ago in Chicago, I began leading a small
group of ten girls, which is a little bit oxymoronic, especially
if you met these girls. There was nothing small about this
group. They were sophomores in high school when I met
them, and I have a theory that sophomore year is one of the

circles of hell, for the sophomores, for their loved ones, and for anyone caught in their path. Freshmen girls are timid and young, and they still have some little girl inside them, and by junior year, they build some identity, some solid blocks of self to stand on, but sophomore year is a free-for-all, one whole year on the verge of disaster, with all the attending emotion and drama and insanity of running with the bulls or of a bad horror movie. Ten sophomore girls in one room multiply somehow, and you could swear there are a hundred of them.

To make matters worse, I couldn't really tell them apart at first. About half of them had almost the same name: Krystina, Christel, Kristin, and Katharine, and Stacey and Stephanie. And they had the adolescent habit of wearing almost identical clothes. It was like they stormed Abercrombie and demanded one in every color, ten hooded sweatshirts, ten pairs of carefully ripped jeans. They were a blur of bright tank tops, flat-ironed hair, and Birkenstock clogs, and I always felt like I was in the middle of a tornado or a high-speed chase.

I didn't actually intend to be their small group leader. I'm not sure they knew that. I worked on the student staff at church, and one year we were short on volunteer leaders for a retreat. I said I could take a group, just for the weekend. Somehow, it was communicated to the girls that I would be their leader forever and ever, and when they found out, they pounced on me and hugged me and jumped up and down, and in that moment I didn't have the heart to say that I had really only agreed to love them for the weekend.

We made it through that weekend, although I called them by the wrong names most of the time, and when we got back, we started meeting every week. And you know, it was okay. I'd prepare a discussion, and then they'd want to spend the whole time talking about tampons. I'd invite them to my house and find one of them going through my cupboards and another going through my trash. They called at all hours of the night and day, and stopped over at my house and my office constantly, and apparently never had anywhere else to be after their visit. They sometimes got so excited to see me that when they hugged me, they knocked me down, even though it was never more than five days since I'd seen them last. There were moments of brilliance, tiny though they were that first year. Sometimes one of them would tell me something that was really true and important about her life. Or one of them would ask me something about life with God that really mattered to her.

To be honest, I planned to make it through one year and then quit, and find a new leader for them in the fall. I worked long hours, and nights and weekends. I was engaged and planning a wedding. They needed so much more than I was prepared to give them—more time, more honesty, more support, more help. But just before the summer, when I planned to quit, something happened. Something happened in me.

Somewhere between going through my trash and asking me about tampons, in between the recitals and games and phone calls, they burrowed into one of the deepest parts of my life and my heart. They became something between friends and little sisters and extensions of my younger selves. They became a central part of my world, my thoughts, my prayers. My schedule became more and more wrapped around their term papers and proms and problems, and my home became more and more the safest landing spot for this strange, whirling little gypsy wagon of girls.

I began to love them, not because they were the finest, most-upstanding kids in our student ministry, because actually they weren't. They had their moments of upstanding-ness, and they had moments of absolute insanity. I loved them because they were mine, because we were us, because of the funny and sweet and strange things they did and said. They're smart and honest and they make big mistakes and dream gorgeous bright dreams. They fall in love hard, sometimes with the right people and sometimes with the wrong people. Sometimes they tell me everything, and sometimes they try not to tell me things, but then the other girls tell me anyway. I think at this point, I know almost all the things they think I don't. And I love them more than they know.

When we left Chicago, leaving them was one of the very hardest things. They changed my life, and I didn't expect them to. I thought it was the right thing to do—to volunteer, to be a mentor, but I was totally unprepared for what was going to happen in my own life. I drove back to Chicago several times that first year, to shop for prom dresses and take pictures before their prom, to go to their graduation and their parties, to see them off as they left for college.

In the last eight years, the eleven of us have lived together through first loves, breakups, parents' divorces, parents' weddings, one mother's cancer, another mother's death, an anxiety disorder, ADD, a learning disability, epilepsy, heartbreak, driver's tests, SATs, one sister's overdose, another sister's suicide, and several funerals of friends. They threw me a wedding shower and put together our wedding programs and helped me throw my mom's fiftieth birthday party. I went to their recitals and plays, and I watched them play powder-puff football, and helped them get ready for dates and cried with them over breakups and failed tests and college rejection letters. We prayed together and sang songs standing next to each other in church, and in some ways their versions of faith were quite young, but in many other much more important ways, they instructed me in matters of practice and theology. They were passionate and articulate and fervent in their prayers, and equally so in their frustration when it seemed like the day-to-day realities of life with God were harder to figure out than they should be.

Now they are graduating from college and dating men they might marry and moving into apartments. We email and talk on the phone. They visit me in Michigan, and when I go back to Chicago for a weekend, we have breakfast at Egg Harbor or coffee at Einstein's.

When I think about how God made us to live, when people talk about true community or true intimacy, I think of them, this lovely, bizarre group of teenage girls who came over unannounced and never left when they were supposed to, who let me into their fears and their secrets, and cared about my fears and my secrets. They loved me with a force that I think only comes with youth, a wide and fierce and expressive force, and I loved them with that same love, because being with them let me live like I was young.

They uncovered something good in me that had started to get crusted over by grown-up life and dress pants and mortgage payments. They taught me more than I ever taught them, and they gave me more than I ever gave them, and the best things they gave to me were ten gorgeous examples and all the permission in the world to love with that wide-open love, unmeasured and uncalculated, like a puppy in a box with all of her puppy-friends, right up close to them, feeling warm and safe.

old house

Until a few years ago, I'd always lived in a new house. But I'd always wanted to live in an old house. I thought of myself as an old-house person, a person who appreciates character over perfection, who likes the bumps and bruises of an old home. So when we moved to Grand Rapids, we bought an old house, an English Tudor built in 1920 with a Hobbit-house sloping roof. I fell in love with it. It has arched doorways and hardwood floors and funny little corners and built-in cabinets. We moved in and started fixing it up, painting, and putting in new outlets and new fixtures.

And then I went over to a friend's house—a new house. I was overcome with jealousy over her new house, not because it was fancy or big, but because the toilets didn't run, and none of the windows were painted shut, and none of the doorknobs get stuck. At our house, there's a doorknob that sticks so emphatically that if my husband's not home to open it, I can't get in. I have to make sure I don't leave anything important in there when he's out of town.

I was so jealous of my friend's new house that when I got back to my house, all I could see were the imperfections, the fixer-upper things that were not yet fixed up. The floors are uneven and the tiles are cracked and the drawers squeak and the radiators clank. We have both bats and mice. The basement smells funny, and I just found some big pieces of the basement ceiling on the floor. I'm not a contractor, but I don't think that's a good sign.

I think of myself as an old-house girl, but I guess there's still a lot of new house in me. I want to love the imperfections, but in a weak moment, I want central air and granite countertops so bad I can't take it. Some of it, unfortunately, is about what other people think. I'm fairly certain that our house is the bad house in the neighborhood, and that our neighbors are whispering to each other disapprovingly every time they drive by.

I was getting ready one morning, putting on makeup and looking out the bathroom window to the street. This woman was driving by very slowly, like she was kind of checking things out, giving us the once-over, and I really had to stop myself from screaming out the window, "We're doing the best we can! We've only been here like five minutes! We're totally unfamiliar with gardening of any kind, and one can only learn so fast!"

But I didn't know that lady. The person having a problem with the house, clearly, is me. And it's not about the house. It's about me. I can't handle any more things that are not quite right in my life, because I feel like that's all I've got. I feel like every single part of my life has bumps and bruises and broken pieces.

I want to be all shiny and new, all put together, and I just can't get there. The things I try to forget don't go away, and the mistakes I've made don't go away, and I'm a lot like my old house, cracked and mismatched and patched over.

On my worst days, I start to believe that what God wants is perfection. That God is a new-house God. That everything has to work just right, with no cracks in the plaster and no loose tiles. That I need to be completely fixed up. I always think that God's kind of people are squeaky-clean people whose garages don't leak, but really a lot of the people God uses to do amazing things are people who don't necessarily have it all together. A lot of the best stories in the Bible, the ones where God does sacred, magical things through people, have a cast of characters with kind of shady pasts, some serious fixer-uppers.

On my very best days, as an act of solidarity with my house, since we're both kind of odd, mismatched, screwed-up things, I practice letting it be an old not-fixed-up house, while I practice being a not-fixed-up person. I wear my ugly pants, the saggy yellow terry-cloth ones with the permanently dirty hems, and I walk around my house, looking at all the things that I should fix someday, but I don't fix them just yet, and I imagine God noticing all the things about me that should get fixed up one day, and loving me anyway and being okay with the mess for the time being.

I practice believing that, bottom line, God loves me as-is, even if I never do get my act together. I put my hand on the plaster wall, nubbly and textured, and I think thankful thoughts about the walls. Then I put my hand on the floor, and I think thankful thoughts about the floor, even though it's scratched and ridged and you can see where one of my black heels lost its little cap and the metal part left tiny round divots in the floor, over and over, like confetti stamped into the wood. I imagine that God does that to me, puts his hand on my head, on my heart, on my savage insecurities, and as he does it, he thinks thankful thoughts about me.

In my best moments, when I calm down and listen closely, God says, "I didn't ask you to become new and improved today. That wasn't the goal. You were broken down and strange yesterday, and you still are today, and the only one freaked out about it is you."

I sometimes hate this house for not being what I want it to be, and I sometimes hate myself for not being that either. But little by little, my funny old broken down house is teaching me that good enough is good enough. Maybe in six months we'll take the home-improvement next step, whatever that might be, and maybe we won't, but my house will keep me warm and dry until then, and I'll try to be kind and gentle to my house and to myself in the meantime.

island

for the Rasmussen family

For more than ten years, our family has been going
to a tiny little island for our family vacations. The island is
four miles long, and there are more stray dogs and chickens
than cars, and the water is the palest aqua you can imagine,
dazzling and surreal. Everything is slightly damp and smells
like salt and rum and french fries, and the roar of the sea
against the island lulls you and makes you feel a million miles
from home, which, for all intents and purposes, we are. We
have no phone and no email, no keys to the little house we
stay in, no car. We leave the windows open so the sea air can
blow through the house, and we ride around in a golf cart
and keep an open tab at the grocery store, so we can just run
in for a package of English ginger nut biscuits or a six-pack
of Coke. There's a small shop that sells us fresh lobster if we
go right when they're bringing them off the boats for the day
and another shop that has gorgeous, gooey baked goods.

We love it there, and there are a million reasons why.
It's the jumble of the waves and the sand and the goats tied
to stakes in people's yards and the shimmering green-blue
of the water and the smell of conch fritters dipped in their

mysterious sauce that I finally discovered is just ketchup and mayonnaise—it's those things that make it magic, that have made it the backdrop of our family's memories for over a decade. It's the almost deafening wind, and the chill in the air at night, and the bands and shop owners and fishermen that we see every year, and the way the clouded sky on the bay looks at sunset, and the mangroves and the stars that are clear and shining like marbles on the road to the club at night.

It's all those things, and something else, the something that our family becomes when we are there. We're the best version of our family there, relaxed and connected and without agenda or schedule. We have conversations that unfold lazily and resolve over days instead of minutes. We tell stories that everyone's already heard, and it doesn't bother us, because we have nothing else to do and nowhere else to be. We're irresponsible, and we make up plans as we go, and we've been going there long enough to have patterns just like worn spots in carpet, patterns that have become traditions, things you do without thinking, that feel familiar and meaningful. The sound of the wind and the barking dogs and the steel drums seem like our sounds, and the taste of conch fritters and rum punch and coconut bread and lobster are our tastes, the taste of vacation, the taste and smell and sound of our family.

We sleep hard because the roar of the waves on the reef keeps us sleeping like babies, and we wake up early, each finding our own spots to read and write and drink coffee before the mildness of the morning burns into the blaze of the day. On vacation, coffee is my dad's culinary contribution, and he takes great pride in measuring the water and the coffee the night before. We eat breakfast on the porch, the screen batted by branches and stalks in the wind, the sun glinting off the water.

We rent a boat every year, and each year it varies from slightly well-loved to downright battered. We snake through the shallow areas, holding our breath, hoping we don't bump the bottom, and we tumble over the side to snorkel when we see a school of fish or a promising reef. It's hot until the sun goes behind the clouds, and then we're all fighting over a few soggy towels because we're covered with goosebumps. When we get back, we take long, hot showers until we shout to each other that the water's going to run out.

At night, we watch movies and eat strange dinners, cobbled together out of whatever we can find at the tiny island store. On New Year's Eve every year, we make as fancy a dinner as we can manage and eat by candlelight on the porch, and we see who can remember where we've spent the New Year each year—Washington D.C., and Minneapolis, and Eagle River, and then ten years here, on this lush, quirky island.

When my brother and I were very small, there was a family from the church that acted sort of like grandparents to us. The family encouraged my parents to begin taking family vacations. My parents had very little time and even less money when we were small, but at the urging of that family, we began a tradition of family vacations. Like many pastors' families, I think, they were borrowed vacations—borrowed Suburbans, borrowed cabins and cottages, borrowed time from the church. And they were great. We have thousands of memories of family time together, thanks to the generosity of many church families.

When the husband and father of the family who first urged us toward vacations died far too young, we sat with his family at his funeral and watched clip after clip of family vacation videos. There were hundreds of photographs and bits of video, funny things and sweet things. You could see the texture of their family through those photographs, and what those images revealed was intimacy and deep love, between a husband and a wife, between parents and children, between grandparents and grandchildren.

When the funeral service was finished, our family stood off to the side for a few minutes before greeting the extended family and friends. My dad had cried a little bit as he spoke at the service, eulogizing his dear friend, but as we stood together, he began to cry in earnest, the chokes and coughs of a man who seldom finds himself so overcome by tears and unable to stop them. He pulled us into a circle, stretching his arms around us.

"We've got to be like that," he choked. "We've got to be like them. We've got to take the time right now because there's nothing more important than this." He bent his head and cried. "We've got to be like that."

Our family vacations since then have carried the weight of that day, and the weight of knowing that one day, our family will mourn the way their family did, and that we want to have the depth and breadth of memories they do. I want my children to know my parents, and not just from emails or short weekend visits. I want my dad to teach them to snorkel someday the same way he taught me, swimming just in front of me with his arm stretched out to the side, letting me hang on that arm and pulling me along with him.

I want to hear every single little thing that my brother has to tell me. Todd is a man of very few words, but every once in a while on vacation he starts talking, while we're taking the golf cart to the club, or putting away the boat at the end of the day. I can badger him via email and cell phone all year long about his life or his girlfriend or his job, and end up knowing very little, but on vacation, sometimes he gets on a roll, and I want to be there when he does, even if it means we sit on the dock till the sun sets and we're freezing, or even if I have to play basketball with him at the court in town.

My mom and dad and brother have grown through the years into my closest friends, the people who tell me the most searing truth, who give me soft places to rest and present to me a bright future when the only one I can see from my vantage point is dim and breaking before my eyes. Families can go either way, and I take no credit for the way we've gone. I accept it like a gift or a winning lottery ticket, and I hold that ticket in my hand tightly, and I take every chance I can get to be with them, for an afternoon, for a weekend, for a vacation, and every moment feels like being given one more winning ticket.

We've invested that small island with as many memories as we can make, crammed it full of love and conversations and stories and long walks and meals and boat rides, because there will be a day when memories are all we have, and I want to know that we have more than we need to last us the rest of our lives. I want to sock away memories like gold coins because I'm going to need them someday to get me through the years.

Vacations are more than vacations, and that island is more than an island. Vacations are the act of grabbing minutes and hours and days with both hands, stealing against the inevitability of time. There will be a day when our family as we know it will no longer exist, and I want to know in that moment that I wasn't at the office or doing the dishes when I could have been walking on the dock with my dad, when I could have been drinking tea and eating ginger cookies on the porch with my mom. I don't want to be building my bank account or my abs or my dream house when I could be dancing with Aaron at the beach bar on New Year's Eve, when I could be making crackers and cheese for dinner because we were on the boat till way after the shops closed, sunburnt and sandy and windblown, and happier there and together than anywhere else with anyone else.

swimming

In the summers during college, I worked at a summer camp. It was shockingly hot and humid, like living in a hair dryer, and smelled like wisteria and swamp water and soap. In the mornings, we tumbled out of bunks and corralled ten tangled heads of hair into ten ponytails on the way to the flagpole, where we said the pledge, wiping sleep from our eyes and crunching pea gravel with our running shoes. All day we zigzagged from our cabins to the dining hall to the archery range to the soccer fields to the zip-line to the pool, always running, letting screen doors slam with a smack. I was hopelessly out of place, with my flat nasal Chicago accent and my kooky California sensibility, an oddity in a wholly Southern world. I learned to two-step and acquired a taste for barbecue.

One of my oldest friends, Tecia, was my co-counselor for several summers. On a hundred hot nights, we sat side by side out on our cabin porch in our pajamas and flip-flops, praying for a little breeze, praying that no one would have a nightmare or wet the bed, telling stories and weaving our lives together, so that by the end of our camp years, if each memory were a snapshot, her face would have been in every frame.

At the end of the term, before taking their kids home, the parents came to watch them compete in a swim meet. So the swim meet was the first time that they would see their kids after having been away from them for a month, which is a really long time if your kids are eight. The pool is decorated with streamers, and the sky always manages to be blue and cloudless. The parents sit in the bleachers and start yelling and waving and taking pictures when the kids come in looking for their parents, waving their tanned arms like windmills on high speed.

All the counselors have jobs for the meet, and some of us are comforters. What that means is that we're assigned to a lane, and we're wearing silly costumes, like a tutu and cowboy boots and a rainbow wig and angel wings, and our whole job is to cheer for whichever girl is in our lane and help her do great in the race.

For one swim meet, I was the comforter in lane five, which is on the far side, away from the parents. It was a long race, several lengths, and the camper in my lane, Jessie, was getting tired. "You're doing great, Jessie," I yelled. "You can make it. Keep going." She had just left the wall on her last length, and I could tell that she was about to start crying. She was tired and the expanse in front of her seemed way too far. She went under for a second, not like she was drowning, but like she was going to give up and turn around. "Look at me, Jessie!" I called. "You're so close! You can make it to me!" She shook her head at me, and she got scared and started to panic and swallowed a big gulp of water, so I jumped in and swam toward her. If she touched me, she would be disqualified, but if she just stayed next to me, knowing that I was there if she needed me, she could make it to the end, and I knew that she wanted to, especially in front of her parents. It would be embarrassing if I rescued her, since she didn't really need it. She just needed someone close enough

to keep her from getting scared again. I swam right next
to her, without touching her, very slowly, and as we swam,
I talked to her in a quiet voice. I said to her, over and over,
"You're tough, Jessie. You're tough and you can make it. I'm
right here, but you can make it." When we got to the end and
she touched the wall, I pulled her out of the water, and she
was so tired, floppy and teary, but the first thing she did was
look up at her mom and wave.

After the meet, I was soaking wet and exhausted, still
wearing a crazy wig and a soggy tutu. Jessie's mom came to
find me as I was closing up the pool. She held my arm and
looked right into my eyes. "Until you have kids of your own,"
she said, "you will never know what this is like. As a mom, all
I wanted to do was run down the bleachers and jump in with
my clothes on to finish that race with my daughter, and I'm so
glad you did. Thank you for caring about my child the way I
would have if I was right there."

That's what friendship looks like to me. Friendship is
acting out God's love for people in tangible ways. We were
made to represent the love of God in each other's lives,
so that each person we walk through life with has a more
profound sense of God's love for them. Friendship is an
opportunity to act on God's behalf in the lives of the people
that we're close to, reminding each other who God is. When
we do the hard, intimate work of friendship, we bring a little
more of the divine into daily life. We get to remind one
another about the bigger, more beautiful picture that we
can't always see from where we are.

Last year, I was at my favorite bookstore. I went there
because I was feeling sort of fragile and overwhelmed,
and one of the things that usually makes me feel better is a
bookstore. I was looking through the cards, the ones that
have quotes on the front, and they're all big, inspirational,

"seize the day"-type quotes, from people like Eleanor Roosevelt and Albert Einstein. If you read them on a good day, you're like, "I will, Eleanor Roosevelt, I will change the world one tiny moment at a time!" But on kind of a cranky, bad day, you read them and you think, "Well, that's why you people are famous, because you do wonderful inspirational things, and all I do is try to get through the day without crying or losing my mind." So I was looking at all these cards, and usually I'm just a sucker for them, but on that night, I felt worn out and hollow. I looked at this whole big wall of cards, and each one was making me feel more broken down and scraped away inside, so far from inspiration and hope. Then I saw one in the corner, in black and white, and it said, "You, too? I thought I was the only one."

And it hit something inside me, and in the card aisle at Schuler's, I started to cry. Really cry, like the kind of tears that have been waiting to come out for a long time. That night I didn't need big, great, beautiful words from important people. I just needed to know that I wasn't alone. "You, too? I thought I was the only one."

True friendship is a sacred, important thing, and it happens when we drop down into that deeper level of who we are, when we cross over into the broken, fragile parts of ourselves. We have to give something up in order to get friendship like that. We have to give up our need to be perceived as perfect. We have to give up our ability to control what people think of us. We have to overcome the fear that when they see the depths of who we are, they'll leave. But what we give up is nothing in comparison to what this kind of friendship gives to us. Friendship is about risk. Love is about risk. If we can control it and manage it and manufacture it, then it's something else, but if it's really love, really friendship, it's a little scary around the edges.

My friend Annette and I met our freshman year in college. She was funny and fun, just as she is now, and she was the real thing, a strong, intuitive, wise person whose words carried serious weight with me, just as they do now. She drove a red Wrangler and seemed to me to be the quintessential California girl. I was certainly the quintessential Midwestern girl in her eyes. She mocked the way I said "maaahm" for "mom" and laughed at my modest one-piece swimsuit.

We became breakfast regulars at the Summerland Beach Café. The first time we went there, I had a gooey cinnamon roll and about two gallons of black coffee, and she ordered the Ranchhand Breakfast, or some such thing, pancakes and eggs and potatoes and bacon. It was enough food for three men, and it cracked me up to see this tiny blonde put away so much food. We routinely went swimming at Cabrillo Beach instead of going to our science class, and we routinely set out to go running and ended up stopping off for margaritas at the beach, or free iced coffees at Starbucks, begged from her friend Javier who worked there.

We always said that sometime we wanted to live in the same town, but she got married and lived in the town she grew up in, and then I got married and lived in the town I grew up in. Three years ago, though, against all odds, she and her husband moved from San Diego to Grand Rapids, partially for a job, partially for a church, and partially because we never stopped talking about what it would be like to really get to be best friends, everyday friends, the kind of friends we can't be when all we have are weekend visits and emails.

The day after Easter, they arrived at our house, Annette and her husband, Andrew, and their ninety-five pound dog, Sydney, and a strange assortment of things, including a large bag of tea and an extremely large bag of spices. Apparently, Annette's mother advised them that moving is costly enough without having all your tea and spices stuck in storage for months and having to buy all new ones. So they each had about two pairs of pants, but all the coriander and Earl Grey they needed.

While they looked for a house, they lived with us. For two months, the four of us and the dog tripped over each other and laughed and told stories and talked about how terrible and hard it is to move. The day they moved into their new house, they left before we were up, and when I went downstairs there was a card from them. When I opened the card, a key slid out, and I started to cry, because this thing, this special, crazy season was over, and they were giving back our key. I thought about how warm and fun and odd our little household was, the four of us trying to make dinner, and talking about old things and new things, and laughing about how messy it was with all of us there. And then I read the card, and it wasn't our house key. It was their new house key. The card said, "You are as much a part of our home as we have been a part of yours."

Nobody would ever recommend having your college roommate and her husband and their dog move across the country and live in your house for two months. But that's that thing, that rare, beautiful thing. Annette shows me over and over that the closer you get to someone, the more that friendship gives you and the more force and power it has to make your life bigger and richer.

Maybe some of what we're doing here is representing the goodness and love of God in tangible ways. You're showing that love to the people in your life and then sometimes they're showing it to you, and when your friend isn't going to make it to the edge of the pool, you jump in with your clothes on and swim next to her.

french class

When I was seven, I wanted to take French lessons. The little school I went to offered them after school, and my friend's mom taught them. I wanted to take those lessons desperately. My mom said I could, but that I had to stick with it, and if I stuck with it long enough, maybe someday I could even go to Paris. I took the classes and loved them. Mrs. Grau was a wonderful, imaginative teacher, and instead of memorizing long lists of nouns and verbs, we learned everything in little units, each based on an experience. We started, I think, with taking an airplane. We learned how to get tickets and how to get boarding passes. We learned the words for suitcase and toothbrush and passport and sweater, all the things one would need for a *voyage*.

When we had learned all the words and phrases, one fabulous day we walked in and she announced to us that it was the day of our voyage— *"Bon Voyage!"* she cried as we walked in. The room was all moved around, and she explained to us that that table was the ticket counter, and that desk was the gate, and through that door was the airplane. We were euphoric and gathered up the little tickets and passports she had made us, and lined up obediently, waiting to say our well-practiced phrases to the ticket agent and the captain and the flight attendant, which were all Mrs. Grau, wearing a sash or a fake mustache or a pin shaped like wings. After our trip, we learned the phrases for dining at a French restaurant, then a trip to the hospital, then to the market, then the rooms of a house. Speaking French seemed like figuring out a puzzle.

Then years later, the week after I finished eighth grade, I boarded a plane by myself and flew from Chicago to Cincinnati to LaGuardia to Frankfurt to Charles de Gaulle in Paris. I felt so grown up and remember thinking that I probably looked like I was about twenty and certainly Parisian. When I look at pictures, however, of my cheery self in front of the Sacré Cœur or at Versailles, I was a chubby blonde girl, wearing a ridiculous blue and white striped sweater with a Liz Claiborne purse and puffy white running shoes, surrounded by slim dark-haired Parisians wearing black.

One of the best things my dad ever said was that he never wanted school to get in the way of my education. I think his dad said that to him, and what it meant was that, among other things, he thought thirteen was definitely old enough to travel alone. I had been traveling with him for years, and when I did, he made sure that I learned, little by little, how to untangle myself from the snags of international travel. Sometimes he would have me check us in, so that I knew how, or figure out which train to take, or who to ask about a hotel. Sometimes he would tell me after a situation had unfolded how to yield better results next time.

When I was twelve, we were at the O'Hare airport, leaving for India and then Europe, and the woman at the gate asked me if I had packed my own suitcase. I said yes. When she asked me if anyone had asked me to carry anything for them, I said, "Yes! In fact, yes! Someone gave me lots of little

packages to carry, and I don't even know what's in them!"
I smiled at the woman behind the counter, thrilled to have
such important news to impart. My father looked at me like I
had turned into a frog. And like he was a little bit angry with
that frog.

After we finally left the gate, after I had unpacked
and unwrapped twenty or so tiny packages of stickers and
lip glosses and glitter pens, leaving paper and ribbons all
over the counter and the floor, my dad mentioned to me, in
a voice that sounded like he was being strangled, that next
time when they ask if anyone has given me anything to carry,
they don't mean one of the church elders giving me a little
package of stickers to open for every day that I'm gone. What
they mean, he continued tightly, is that if a man you've never
met lures you into a dark corner and forces you to put a box
wrapped in brown paper making ticking noises into your bag,
that's what they're talking about. He was walking really fast
toward our gate, and I had to break into a little run to keep up
with him. "Got it," I said, out of breath from trotting alongside
him. "Can you believe how cute those stickers are?"

On that flight to Paris a year later, I rehearsed my
phrases and gripped my little case with my passport and
credit card and tickets like they were my best friends. When
I arrived at Charles de Gaulle, I found my rolling suitcase and
the map I had marked and walked across the bridges toward
the apartment where I would stay. My parents had a friend
who was an artist in Paris, and she agreed to let me stay with
her for a week. What we hadn't really discussed before I left
was the fact that in exchange for rent, she answered the
phones in her building all day, so, really, if there was anything
I wanted to see in Paris, I was going to have to find it alone.

So I did. Every morning she brought me chocolat
chaud and a bit of a baguette, and we spread out the map

on the floor and made lists of all the places Mrs. Grau had taken me to in our little classroom with her fake mustaches and berets. It was magical. It was like reading *Alice in Wonderland* a thousand times and then actually falling down the rabbit hole. All day I tromped around, on the metro and on the bus and over the bridges, to the Musee D'Orsay and the Place des Invalides and the Centre Pompidou. I ate crepes with Nutella for every meal because I was thirteen and there was no one around to stop me. I walked the tall steps at Montmartre and Sacré Cœur and wandered by the street artists and vendors there, rehearsing my phrases furiously several times before I blurted them out all in one breath—"I like your painting!" or "What a pretty dog!"

I know I was happy before that, that there were things that made me happy. I loved to dance and loved to swim, but there was something that happened to me on that trip. It began a love affair, specifically with Paris, but even more with traveling, and more than that, traveling alone. I felt so small and so anonymous, surrounded by the sounds and smells and sights of a place I'd only read about, and I could go as quickly or as slowly as I wanted to. There are only two things I like to do alone: reading and traveling, and for the same reason. When you travel, and when you read, you are not actually alone, but rather surrounded by other worlds entirely, the footsteps and phrases of whole other lives keeping you company as you go.

It's pretty easy to fall in love with Paris, but Paris was just the beginning for me. I've become, since that trip, an equal-opportunity solo traveler. I love Pittsburgh and Hamburg and Pismo Beach. I love Ann Arbor and Austin and Evanston. I love the tacos at La Superica on Milpas in Santa Barbara and the smell of waffle cones on Water Street in Saugatuck. And I love them best by myself. I've been to Paris several times since then, and each time I am there, I think of that first time, of my very young self, and the first time I felt the perfect happiness of being alone in a magical place.

It felt like being at a fancy hotel's breakfast buffet, where you're so overwhelmed by the options, you almost want to give up, but more than overwhelmed, you are delighted, and you want to taste every single bite, and just walking up to the stack of plates makes you feel like something great is happening to you. That's how it feels to be alone in a city, like something great is always about to happen to you. And it always is. There's always some side street or café or painting in a gallery or park or person or something that takes your breath away. And you look differently when you're alone. When you're with someone else, you share each discovery, but when you are alone, you have to carry each experience with you like a secret, something you have to write on your heart, because there's no other way to preserve it.

carrying my own weight

I loved to dance when I was little, but at a certain point I stopped taking lessons because I was so tired of always being the biggest one, needing the biggest costume or uniform, holding my breath and sucking in my stomach, hoping there would be one that fit me.

I wanted to look like my mother and her mother—small, dark-haired, fine-boned, like blackbirds or Russian princesses. Instead, I looked like I belonged in a Breughel painting, a Dutch peasant in a field. I looked like I could be cast in the "Beef: it's what's for dinner" commercials, and all I wanted to be was a fine black-winged bird.

Some of my most horrifying memories involve trying to find something to wear to an event my parents were taking me to, when I was chubby and adolescent and somehow chronically between sizes. I always ended up in some cobbled together, safety-pinned thing, feeling like an impostor. Getting dressed was always a blistering, painful affair, exacerbated by the fact that the primary person helping me through this ordeal was my size-two mother, who had a knack for saying things like, "Hmmm . . . is that a little tight?" *Is it a little tight, Mom?* Yes. Yes, it's a little tight.

Everything I've ever tried on has been a little tight. My whole life feels a little tight.

Being too big was a vulnerability for me, a liability, something that made me an outsider. And being too big certainly did not help my dating life. There was the fateful phrase I've heard a thousand times: *You're just like a sister.* Or slightly better, I guess: *You're not the kind of girl you date—you're the kind of girl you marry.* Which, now that I am married, is a compliment, but when you're fifteen and all you want to do is get asked to homecoming, being marriage material is as cool as having a good personality. Who wants a good personality when you could have a cute butt?

Birthdays have always been especially hard for me because I've always believed that by this one, okay, now by this one, I'll be my new self, and I never am, and there is a moment when I'm alone at my own party, in the ladies room or in the kitchen, where I am blinded by a flash of sadness for what I will drag into the next year, poisoning it and weighing it down. And then I dredge up the hope again and tell myself that this is the year, this one. By my next birthday, it will be different. That's what I say every year, and every year I believe it, and every year it is a lie.

I spent lots of time shopping and planning so that I would always have the right things to hide behind. I watched my friends shop for fun, and it was as foreign as breathing underwater. I shopped as defense. I had pages and pages torn out of the J.Crew catalog of the clothes I would buy once I was thin. And as I shopped, I planned and dreamed for what I thought my life would be like when I was thin. I knew that it would be better, easier. But that life never came.

In high school, I tried to control myself like the anorexics I knew, but I always gave in. After a day or two days or a week of being good, of being precise and measured and powerful, I always lost control and ate cake that I had put in the freezer so that I wouldn't eat it, or pounds and pounds of peanut butter cups, until I was numb and hysterical and angry at my body all over again.

I knew the magic of bulimia was that you could eat and eat and then just throw up to get rid of it, instead of getting up at five in the morning to stairmaster for an hour, which was getting harder and harder for me. For a while, there was a little voice inside me that said making myself throw up was really over the line, and that a little dieting was one thing, but bulimia was another. At that point, I had already put myself on an entirely liquid diet and had been living on broth, black coffee, and sugar-free lime Jell-O. I'm not sure why throwing up seemed all that extreme.

The summer I was fifteen, I was at our cottage alone one day and had an idea. Summer was always particularly hard for me because of all the time at the beach and at camp, and because I always felt the expectation, the ticking clock, that soon I would go back to school and this would be the year that I would finally be skinny, and that I would finally be happy.

I learned in health class that if you drink poison, you should drink Syrup of Ipecac to get the poison out of your stomach. So I rode my bike to the drugstore in town and bought a tiny bottle of it and a gallon of ice cream. I figured for my first time, I wanted to throw up something soft and melty, like ice cream, instead of, for example, steak or Chex Mix. I ate a whole bunch of the ice cream, and then I took a bit of the syrup, the recommended dosage. I waited ten minutes or so, and was worried that maybe I took the infant amount, so I swallowed another little bit. And within another ten minutes, something totally beyond description happened in that cottage and in my body. Throwing up is horrible, but if regular throwing up is like putting a car into reverse, this was like putting a car into reverse and hitting a hundred miles an hour backward. It was otherworldly and scary.

I threw up for hours, and it was like my body was a fire hose, and the force of what was coming out tossed me around like a doll. It was gross and painful, and I had to clean up the cottage for hours, because I kept thinking I was finally finished, and then without notice, would throw up some more. When it was finally over, I laid on the ground, my throat raw and totally exhausted.

And I did it again. You would think that I learned my lesson, that the horror of it put me off, and I saw the error and sickness of my ways. No. I did it a few more times, with similarly superhuman results, and each time I did it, it felt like some sort of cosmic battle, like I might vomit out my soul, but I also felt powerful and in control, which is something I never felt about my body. After a few times, though, I started to get scared and went back to tamer ways of abusing my body, like only eating at night, or only eating fat-free Cool Whip and mandarin orange Diet Rite.

It didn't occur to me then that there was a way to live in my body, my too-big body, without shame and abuse. It seemed like it was my responsibility to punish it, and that if I had been kind to it, that would have been permitting or sanctioning its disobedience. I believed, literally and figuratively, that if I released my hold on it, released the hatred and the pressure by an inch, it would expand, I would expand, like rising dough, like cupcake batter puffing up and spilling over onto the pan.

What I wanted more than anything was to not have a body. This body that I dragged around had been my enemy for so long and had betrayed me so deeply, over and over, by having the audacity to be fat. I hated it, the particular and venemous way you hate someone you used to love, someone who was supposed to be on your side and wasn't, and who was in fact, fighting against you.

I was a spirit and a mind unfortunately trapped in rather bad packaging, like a bad ad campaign for a genuinely good product. I felt strongly misrepresented by my body, like when you put a silver ring in a toaster-oven box and wrap it, and then the person thinks they're getting an appliance, but they're really getting a ring. I felt like my body was inaccurate in its representation of me, and that made me furious with it.

After two decades of frustration and shame, these days, owing to several small and large miracles, for the first time in my life, I am less than hateful toward my body, and in shining moments, even quite kind to it. Month by month, I work hard to see it less and less as this other thing, this distant distinct shell, and more like a nice person that I might like to be friends with. The last few years have felt like traveling back a cosmic distance to rejoin these two entirely separate entities, my spirit and my body.

I don't know if it was the sum of several things coming together, or if it was my age, or God's graciousness and that all my prayers over two decades finally landed in the right inbox, or that I lost my baby fat later than all the other babies, but at a certain point, I lost weight. After a year of hard work and gradual, incremental change, all of a sudden, there I was, there at the place I had imagined all my life. I shopped for fun and even started assuming things would fit. I shared clothes with my girlfriends and my mom, and felt like I finally joined a sorority I'd been barred from. I stopped having panic attacks in dressing rooms. I ordered things online, and they fit, with no alterations. In the course of a year or so, I became a person who can get dressed without crying, a person who can go swimming without a boatload of self talk.

I thought a lot of things would get easier instantly. And some have. But many haven't. I thought, of course, that this was the key that would turn all the locks inside me, that would set in motion all the parts of my life that seemed stuck and stalled. I thought seeing that magic, fabled, dreamt-of number on the scale would turn me into a person who revels in her own skin, who dances in her underwear, who walks into every room fearlessly and shamelessly. I thought that number on the scale would protect me from the vulnerability I had always felt, that it would secure me, once and for all, a place at the cool kids' table at lunch, my very own place in the world of successful, happy, confident people.

What I found, though, is that if you're not chasing one fantasy, you're chasing another. If it's not your body, it's your bank account, and if it's not your bank account, it's your résumé or your nose or your boobs or your car or the perfect marriage or the perfect vacation or the perfect child. For two decades, I believed that if I could just get this one thing under control, then the whole of my life would magically bloom like a perfect, lush flower. But to my great dismay, I realized that my life was still my life, and I was still myself, just in smaller pants.

Certainly, there was a particular joy I felt in those smaller pants. For a person who had routinely cried in dressing rooms, those new sizes made me childishly, inexplicably happy. But what I found is that there is no such thing as skinny enough. There is no magic number that can make you feel safe or protected or confident. That, I found, was an entirely different thing—a belief, a decision, something—but not a number.

I became confident the cheap way, at first, by Zone-dieting myself down to a cuter butt and into smaller pants. But after a while, I found that the cheap stuff wasn't going to do it anymore, and I needed the real thing, the ever-elusive thing: peace. Peace with the way I was made, with the self I was given, with the way life is unfolding around me, but more specifically, with the way it is unfolding in my arms and my legs and my mouth and my eyes.

And that required an entirely different language and set of practices. Yoga is one. It's helped to connect the inside me to the outside me, to bind my breath and my thoughts and my arms and legs into one whole, as opposed to bright spirit and faulty shell. I know it's so five years ago to discover yoga. But when yoga was new and cool, I was still hating my body with such venom, that all that kind, empathetic, thankful yoga business was downright offensive to me.

I've had to rethink and relearn a thousand things, about food and silence and judgment and walking. In the words of the Indigo Girls, whom I love and feel I am close personal friends with, psychically, it's about learning to "starve the emptiness and feed the hunger."

The biggest change, though, to my surprise, isn't in my body, but in my eyes—the cruel, appraising, critical eyes that have been measuring and accusing my body for decades. And in my mind. I couldn't forget if I tried what my life was like before that, feeling like a linebacker in a world of Tinkerbells, the pinching feeling of a too-tight waistband making my stomach feel fleshy and soft, like scrambled eggs spilling over the top of my pants.

I carry with me the very heavy shame of being ten and too big, and fifteen and too big, and twenty and too big, and twenty-five and too big. And it's a lot to carry, but I can't leave it behind. I don't want to. In some ways, everything has changed, and at the same time, when I look into my own eyes in the mirror, we both know that only so much has, and that we all carry our own weight in very different ways.

these are the days

When I was twenty, I spent a semester traveling through England, Ireland, and Scotland with twenty-odd (*odd*, certainly, being the operative word) English and theater majors, seeing lots of live theater, reading Hardy in Hardy Country and Austen in her hometown and so on. It was as strange and fantastic as it sounds, complete with extremely quirky thespians, obscure-poetry-quoting literati, and innumerable hours on a coach.

Before the semester abroad, I knew a few of them from classes, friends of friends, acquaintances, but over the course of the trip, six of us became a little family. We became a tight little band of troublemakers, brothers and sisters, witnesses to several months of stories that our friends at home would never believe if we told them. Now we are adults, ostensibly, some of us mothers and fathers, one a PhD, one in real estate, one in PR. We dip into one another's lives in Seattle, Boston, and San Francisco, when business takes us to one another's cities, or when we gather for weddings and to celebrate babies. But back then, a thousand lifetimes ago, a thousand selves ago, we were six young American travelers, stumbling and crashing through

Europe, falling in and out of love with it, with one another, with ourselves.

Kirsten was the eldest of our little family, blonde and gorgeous and expressive. She played the guitar and her laugh sounded like thin sheets of glass breaking. I wanted to be like her in every possible way. The nuns at the house we lived in referred to Mark as the Usual Suspect. He was tall and couldn't escape their attention. He was smart and funny, with long dark hair. He became my best friend, my accomplice, and almost every one of my memories of those months include him. Monica was the achiever of the group—must-see and must-do lists for every city, itemized, prioritized, and mapped. If it weren't for her, several wonders of the world would have been skipped in favor of cocktails. She was the sunniest, easiest going of us. Sara was the mysterious one, dark-haired and so smart it kind of freaked us out. She slept like a cat, hard and often, sprawled out all hours of the day. And Ryan, her partner in crime, was blond and incisive and honest and wondrously strange.

We began in Edinburgh, still one of my favorite cities. We went to shows at all hours of the night and day, and because we were in the right place at the right time, looking sufficiently American, we got invited to a party inside the castle, which sounded so glamorous, but was unfortunately a dim pub in the bowels of the castle, populated by a downtrodden regiment of the Royal Scottish military who wanted us to sit on their laps. I'm afraid we disappointed them.

Our home base was Hengrave Hall, a sprawling fifteenth-century manor house in the middle of absolutely nowhere. It was gorgeous and damp and seemed like the kind of place that would be haunted. I lived in the East chamber with Kirsten and Sara and Monica, and the distinction of that chamber was that it was directly above the kitchen, meaning that we were able to enjoy the scent of, for example, boiled fish, many hours before and many hours after mealtime. For breakfast, we had gallons of tea, heavily sugared, and stacks of toast, and for lunch, something British-y—and by that I mean warm, mushy, and salty—with dessert, a cake or crumble over which we poured warm custard. Lots and lots of warm custard. I'm certain that warm custard alone accounted for the dozen extra pounds I brought home as a souvenir.

Living at Hengrave was sort of like living in a British novel and sort of like being sick. Because we were there for stretches of several days at a time, and the nearest town was several miles away, we padded around in slippers and sweatshirts clutching novels and cups of tea, like well-read invalids.

On warmer days, we explored the grounds, the orchards, the gardens, and the tiny stone chapel, and on nights when we stayed out so late that they locked the doors, and our roommates didn't respond to the rocks we threw at their windows, we slept in the unheated summerhouse and sneaked back into the main house in the morning. We memorized long passages of Shakespeare while perched on radiators because of the chill, and many of the girls learned to knit, dragging around balls of yarn like lifeless cats. For those and many other reasons, it seemed that we may have slowly been going crazy.

But every so often, to stem the rising tide of insanity, and to see some great and not-so-great shows, we'd go to London or Dublin or Bath, and set up camp anew at a bed and breakfast. We stayed at one in Oxford that had a glass shower right in the room, next to one of the beds. We felt slightly better, noticing that the glass was frosted in the center, providing a touch of very necessary modesty, but our hopes were dashed when we realized that the frosted section covered approximately ribs to hips, and consequently none of the important parts.

One of the reasons I went on the trip was that my favorite professor, Heather, was teaching the semester course. When I left for the trip, of course, I would never ever have called her Heather, and even still it feels a little weird, like calling your mom by her actual name. My professor Heather was and is one of the clearest real-life pictures of the kind of person I want to be.

When I was eighteen, I took her class in my first semester of college at Westmont. She was impossibly articulate and intelligent. She pushed us and made us want to impress her and please her, so we studied hard and wrote voraciously and read very carefully, hoping to bring her something of value to each class meeting, like small children cupping fireflies and salamanders in their hands. She became my advisor, and then my friend. I was a daughter far away from my mother in Chicago, and Heather's daughter had gone away to college that same year. We talked about books and about telling the truth in your writing, and she told me about how she met her husband, how he was a professor when she was a student. It was slightly scandalous and made her seem even more glamorous. She was beautiful and strong and tall with blonde hair, and she wore several thin gold rings on one finger.

When I moved to Santa Barbara, and out of my parents' home, Heather gave me another image of how to be a woman. I needed my mother's image, but I also needed a few more images with which to piece together a future self. Heather is one of the most significant of those images. She pushed me, as a writer and as a person of faith and as a woman. There were times when I failed her, and when I did, her disappointment crushed me, and then her grace healed me. I think she thought I was smart, and possibly special, and I think she saw something of herself or maybe her daughter in me. Maybe not. Maybe she was just a really good teacher who let me hang around the English department, looking for myself.

During one of our extended stays at Hengrave, Mark and I walked into town one afternoon to find a scenic place to sit while we memorized our poetry passages. We thought the train platform was picturesque, and after we watched a few trains arrive and depart, bored with our poetry, we decided that we should definitely take one. We asked the man behind the ticket window where he would go if he were us, and we took his advice and bought tickets to Great Yarmouth, a funny old-time resort town on the coast. We tried to call the house to tell them we were staying there for the night, but the line was busy a few times, and apparently we thought it wasn't that big a deal. We ate pizza and drank red wine at a basement Italian restaurant with checkered tablecloths, and found rooms the size of linen closets on the top floor of a bed-and-breakfast. In the morning, we drank espresso and wandered around a street market before catching the train home.

It turns out that our spontaneous trip was, in fact, a very big deal. When we walked in, we could tell by the way everyone was looking at us and then looking over at Heather, who was not smiling, that it was a very big deal. We tried to make it kind of a funny vaudevillian tale, and used big hand gestures and a fair amount of slapstick, telling them about how we just happened to be at the train station and just happened to pick Great Yarmouth. We traded off telling about how we stopped at a little grocery store for

notebooks, pens, and ice cream for the train, and about how
the street market had super gross butcher sections, with
whole skinned animals all hanging in a row like Noah's Ark
gone terribly wrong. Our friends were amused, but Heather,
clearly, was not.

She asked me to take a walk with her, and after we
walked a bit, we sat on a bench with our backs to the house,
looking out over the black branches in the fading light.
She was worried about me, she said. She was worried that
although I thought I was, in Tennyson's words, "drinking life
to the lees," I might be missing some of the most important
parts. She said that she loved to hear my stories, about
taking trains and staying out all night and drinking with
strangers and swimming in fountains, but that she feared I
was losing my ability to be contemplative. She told me that
I was a leader, and that the other students would follow me,
and that she didn't think I was leading them anywhere worth
going.

Her words mattered to me. Her opinion of me
mattered to me. I wrote down her exact words that day in my
journal, and while they were completely accurate then, they
were also prophetic: as I grow older, I am able to see that
same pattern throughout my life. When I am at my best, I can
see and think and feel at a deep level, and when I am at my
worst, I'm a tap-dancing, tipsy show-off, with funny stories
and hand gestures and painfully little else.

On the first day of the trip, in Edinburgh, this was
Heather's prayer: "Help us to be brave with one another,
for these are the days." She was right. They were the
days. They were singularly beautiful, terrible days. In some
ways, I was never more myself, and in others, never more
unrecognizable. But we were brave with one another, which
is, I'm finding, more than one can ask for. She was brave with

me, telling me the truth about myself, and I think I was a little bit brave with her, withstanding her disappointment and letting it reach down to the deepest parts of me and draw me up to a better self.

visions and secrets

I can remember my mom saying years and years ago
that I should think about writing, because it might be one
possible use for the sheer amount of things that go on in
my mind at any given time. I wondered if that was true,
and hoped for that, and then at a certain point had almost
stopped hoping for that, because I had found my place, I
thought. I had found use and stability in another world, a
world of people and ideas and teams and meetings, but what
I wanted to be, in a dreamy far-off way, was a writer.

When I think about my child-self, my little girl
memories, all that little girl wanted to be was a storyteller,
a poet, a person who gathers and arranges words like
some people gather and arrange flowers. Words are
the breakdown through which I see all of life, instead of
molecules or notes or chords or colors. Words in even black
and white snakes, back and forth across the page, the portals
through which a little girl found a big world, and through
which, now, a grown-up girl is trying to pass.

When I write, I can see things that I can't otherwise see,
and I can feel things that I can't otherwise feel. Things make
sense, in flashes and glimpses, in me and around me. They

unravel themselves and line up into black and white rows, and those rows nourish me, sliding down my throat like noodles.

When I write, about half an hour breezes by usually, and then it all screeches to a halt like cars crashing. I get stuck, convinced it was a bad idea to even start. *Start where you're stuck.* That's what my (genius) therapist, who is also a writer, told me. A little piece of me wanted to scream at him that I don't think I pay seven dollars a minute for him to give me the same writing advice that I could find in every book on writing on my shelf, but, come to think of it, he was right, and I was stuck, and I had been crying for the better part of an hour. I get stuck because I try to map out every dip and turn, try to write an ending, literally and figuratively, before a beginning even exists. So I don't write, but with the energy that I could use on writing, I worry instead. There is a blanket of depression and anxiety and frustration covering over everything, and I blame anything within striking distance — specifically, the usual suspects of my husband, our house, and the entire town of Grand Rapids, both its inhabitants and its civil offerings.

After I'm through ranting and raving at my poor husband and listing for him, again, all the reasons we need to move, I realize tragically that I still feel the sadness and terror, and that I did not, in fact, solve my problem. So it wasn't Aaron, it wasn't the house, it wasn't the town. It's the fear and the chaos and the strange and wonderful and entirely new thing unfolding in me.

I am stunned, still, and keep marveling at it. Six months ago, even, things were murky, tangled, and teary. I knew that something in me was changing, but it felt vague and not-yet-here, like a low train whistle or a growl of thunder in the distance. I've spent a hundred nights trying to find words for what's happening, feeling something strange and new being born.

I started to get tiny glimpses of the writing life I always wanted, shimmering and bright, but I was living this other life, one that I had come to love, or at least to expect. Quitting my job to write a book seemed as realistic as moving from Grand Rapids to the moon, so I hung in the half-place, dreaming about one and plugging away at the other. I hid behind my job because it was safer, and because I genuinely felt passionate about the work I was doing. I wasn't a waitress/actress toiling away with a coffee pot until my big break. I loved my church and loved working there. I loved the people I worked with. It's the only work I've ever done, and the only thing I felt prepared and experienced to do. It's my first language, my native tongue; and writing, while it feels so beautiful and dreamy, also feels awkward, like a second language or a new yoga pose.

I kept finding myself in tears, hoping for a life that was wholly different from the one I was living. I couldn't figure out if I was just tired and needed a vacation, or if I was scared and needed to quit. Everyone has dreams that they think about on bad days at work. But they're dreams, right? You don't actually do them, right? You get back to work. So that's what I did.

But sometimes at my desk I let emails and phone calls go unanswered for a minute, and sometimes I drove in silence in my car, waiting for something, hoping for something to break through, crack through, and connect the dots that felt scattered all over my life. I prayed a lot in the middle of the night, prayers that sounded more like sobs, not at all sure what I was even asking for.

And now I can feel things turning, slowly. I can feel this tiny, fragile writer person getting bigger, like a candle flame growing. Tonight is a writing night, and I feel giddy, antsy, bold in a new way. I feel like I have a secret: I am becoming something else. On the outside, I look like a person who has a desk and meetings, but underneath, I'm a writer. I'm a writer. I keep saying it to myself, and it feels risky and furtive.

For me, to write is an act of rebellion, an uprising against that part of me that needs to be responsible, helpful, adaptive. It is one of the first things, maybe the very first thing, that is entirely my own, that doesn't help anyone, doesn't make anyone else's life easier, doesn't facilitate or provide structure or administrative support for anyone else. I've always been a team player, a utility player, a workhorse, and to do something sheerly out of a deep love for the act itself feels foreign and vaguely scandalous. It feels, I'm realizing, selfish.

But little by little, when I start where I'm stuck, over and over and over, getting stuck and unstuck, something cracks through, and life reveals itself to me like a scroll unfurling, and I write about it. I struggle against myself, and I write about it. I feel afraid and crazy, and I write about it. I don't figure out the solution in any tidy way, and I don't have a sharp and clever revelation, but bit by bit, writing is starting to worm its way into the dailiness of my life and is creating a home there. It is becoming less and less of a strange distant dream and more and more of the actual way I live.

I feel, in the best moments, in spite of the uncertainty, in spite of the fear, like Lily Briscoe in *To the Lighthouse*. *Yes, she thought, laying down her brush in extreme fatigue, I have had my vision.* I had that line written on my wall for years, years ago, and now it holds a whole new richness. I have had my vision, and I thought it would come in a flash, a bright beam of knowing. But it has come in the same way that all things come to me. It has come to me with a fight. It has come to me the hard way, through tears and fog and fear and chaos, and now has landed in the palm of my hand like a firefly. There now, I have had my vision.

II

baby making

Aaron and I had decided in the fall that after we went on a trip in November, it would be baby-making time. We had been married for four years, were about to turn thirty, and had done all of those things we said we wanted to do before we had kids. We were extremely and satisfyingly irresponsible. We ate lots of takeout. We took last-minute trips and decided to extend our stays without having to call a sitter or a school. We worked long hours and weekends and nights, throwing ourselves into projects and plans. We worked on holidays and never had a Christmas tree. We bought silly things like TiVo and expensive jeans, and we threw lots of parties, and all of a sudden we realized that we had done all those things we were so intent to do before baby time.

When we got back from that trip, and the moment came to actually not take that tiny pill, I was the one who got cold feet and said, "Ooh, maybe just one more month." And Aaron, who had been specifically terrified of this moment for years, all of a sudden proved himself a family man and said, "No, it's time. We're ready." And off we went, into the unknown of "Are we or aren't we having a baby?"

One Wednesday in January, I realized I was all the things they tell you to be on the lookout for—hungry, tired, weepy, odd—but I made myself not take a pregnancy test just yet. Actually, Aaron made me not take a test just yet. He said that we'd spend that baby's college fund on pregnancy tests if every time I "felt" pregnant, I took a nine-dollar test. He knows me all too well. So I waited until Thursday night, which felt like a million years, and when I took the test, there was a tiny, ever so faint plus sign. I showed it to Aaron while he was watching TV, and he said that that wasn't a plus sign, that was where a plus sign *would* be, and that we'd hope for a positive result next month. But I had heard people say that positive was positive, even if it was faint. And if I really squinted, I could definitely see a plus sign. He made me promise not to take any more tests that night, so I only took one more while he was still watching TV, but I did it wrong, so I don't think that counts. I had one more test left for morning, when these things are supposed to be easier to discern, and thankfully, it was one of the digital tests that would actually say "pregnant" or "not pregnant."

The next morning, I had planned to stop over at my friend Ruth's house. I set my alarm to make it to Ruth's before she took her son Oskar to preschool, and when the alarm went off, I saw the last test on the nightstand. I took it and climbed back in bed with Aaron to wait. "Pregnant," it said. Distinctly, plainly. I showed it to Aaron, who became wide awake very quickly and said, "Stay here. You can't leave me at a moment like this." I called Ruth and gave her some odd excuse for which I apologized later. It seems like there would be so many things to say in that moment, but Aaron and I found ourselves silenced under the enormity and shock of it. We laid side by side in the bed, staring at the ceiling, amazed and afraid.

For the first twelve weeks, I slept most of the time, and I ate the rest of the time. And then, just like everyone promised, at twelve weeks it was like the fog lifted, and I felt like myself again. Myself, only fatter. A lot fatter. The two most traumatized areas were my thighs and my knees. Something terrible happened in that region, and I'm just choosing to believe it's reversible.

One of my best friends gained over eighty pounds with her first pregnancy. A friend of hers said later that now knowing her son, it makes sense, those eighty pounds, because it really may have taken all that space to contain his whole self, his big, grand spirit inside of her. I think that's a lovely way to look at it, and I keep telling myself that maybe our little one needs a little more room to wiggle than the average bear, just like my friend's son did.

I like to keep that explanation in mind when I try to find maternity clothes that actually look good, but there's only so much you can do with huge elastic panels and empire waists. I always end up feeling like an oversize child. And I know I'm not making it easy on those maternity clothes. I am not an only-pregnant-in-her-belly kind of pregnant. I'm pregnant in my face and my hands and feet and arms. My nose is pregnant.

What I didn't expect was that right from the beginning, the baby would occupy so much of my mind and spirit. I knew it would occupy my body, but I was surprised by how deeply it took root in my thoughts and prayers and dreams. I was never unaware of it. I never forgot about it, never woke up surprised by my big belly. It is much more an active thing than I thought, a thing to do, to care for, to think about. I thought it happened to you, and then at some point a baby came and that's when the life change began. But that's not the case at all.

At our five-month appointment, we had our first ultrasound and found out that we're having a boy. Everyone from the lady at the video rental place to my good friends thought it was a girl, because of the way I was carrying, because I wasn't sick, because of how my ankles looked. The night before the ultrasound, Aaron and I laid in bed and both said we thought it was a girl, and we were getting used to the idea.

So when the ultrasound technician told us that definitively, certainly, it was a boy, we were shocked and quiet. And thrilled. We had picked the name Henry for our first boy years ago, and in the car on the way home from the doctor, we decided that yes, that's his name, Henry Niequist. When Aaron leaves for work these days, he kisses my belly and says, "Henry, this is your dad. Be good for your mom today. I love you."

I felt Henry move for the first time just after the ultrasound, a tiny flutter while I was standing at the kitchen counter looking through the mail. Now he moves almost constantly, sometimes diving and twisting so dramatically that I feel like I'm on a roller coaster and my stomach drops.

One of the best things about being pregnant, I think, is how vividly I taste and feel and smell things. A soft chair can truly make me believe that all is right with the world, and sweet corn and ripe peaches just annihilate me with their flavor. Lavender soap can make me almost pass out with happiness. I have never been so easily and deeply satisfied.

The reverse, unfortunately, is also true. Uncomfortable shoes feel specifically engineered to torture me, and there is nothing worse than the smell of raw chicken or mildew. A friend of mine who was recently pregnant said she could smell a person's breath from a mile and a half away.

When I think beyond the pregnancy, about this actual person, this tiny baby-person in our house, there are a million things I am afraid of, of Henry falling or drinking some cleaning product I didn't have child-locked away. I'm afraid of him being afraid, of him being sad, of him being the kid that smells a little bit like pee all the time. I'm afraid of not ever having the natural mom instinct kick in, afraid of what all these changes will do to our marriage, afraid that I will be a controlling mom who can't let her kids live their own lives. I'm afraid I'll get into a car accident with the baby in the car, or that I'll fall down the stairs with him.

But at the same time, something inside me, maybe the hormones or the grace of God, something keeps telling me that of all the things I can't do and will never be, that I can do this one. I can be a mother. Aaron and I can be a family. It feels, in some moments, like our whole histories have been leading us toward this.

In some ways, it's just waiting. Waiting and preparing. But in other ways, it feels like having a secret all your own, something precious to carry around with you, like knowing about a surprise party no one else knows about, like having a tiny friend with you all the time.

I can't wait to meet this little person, to see his eyes and his face, to see whose face we see in his, Aaron's or my dad's or my brother's. I can't wait to tell him about all the things we did together when I was pregnant, about going to Zurich and Orlando and Harbor Springs and Chicago, about how much we started loving him the moment he existed, and how much he has changed our lives even now. About how I walked around and around the neighborhood, thinking about the nursery, rubbing my belly, trying to tell him that we will take care of him the very best we can.

I don't know what the future holds. I don't know what I'll do and what I won't do in my life. But I can tell already that baby making is going to be one of the very best things I do. And Henry-making is my proudest accomplishment yet.

So come on, Henry Niequist. Come on into our lives and our home and our hearts. Change us, invade us, turn us inside out. Come on in. Come on out.

the red tree

A few months ago, in the golden crackle of fall, I woke
up early on a Friday morning. I was getting a cold. That
month, we hosted a baby shower, a wedding shower, and a
rehearsal dinner at our house. I made a job transition at the
church, which we all know means you work two entire jobs
for a while, and call it a transition. A good friend got married,
another celebrated her thirtieth birthday, another found
out she's pregnant, and another adopted a newborn. My
husband had his wisdom teeth removed, because we had so
much extra time that month for elective surgery, and on this
particular Friday morning, I was two weeks from teaching at
an event, and had no idea what I was going to say, or what
I was going to wear, both of which were causing me just a
teeny bit of stress.

My husband needed more gauze for his teeth, and
more ice cream, and more soup, and while I was going, more
strawberries. Okay.

I threw a coat over my pajamas, flew out the door, and
raced through the store, throwing things in the cart. On the
way home, I had a phone conversation that totally stressed
me out about one of the upcoming events. When I got

home, my husband told me that I bought the wrong gauze. You would think I could get the right gauze because I had already bought it seven times that week, but it was indeed the wrong gauze.

I didn't even let him finish what he was saying. I stomped out the door, back into the car, still in my pajamas, and as I opened the garage door again, I stopped in my tracks. In the park across the street, one of the tallest trees, twice as high as a two-story house, was the brightest, most insane, lit-from-within red I have ever seen. And it took my breath away, for two reasons.

First, because it was so beyond beautiful, and second, because I had not noticed one step of its turning. I had been in and out of my driveway a zillion times in the last two weeks and could not have told you if the tree was even still standing or not. As I stood there in the driveway, I realized that I had stopped seeing the most important things to see.

I saw the to-do list, the accumulation of things in the house that would have to be shoved in closets for the parties. I saw the stack of half-finished ramblings and Post-Its all over my desk that were not turning themselves into a brilliant talk like I hoped they would. I saw the pile of things to go to the dry cleaner and the pile of work to be done and the pile of promises I had made and couldn't possibly keep.

I saw the long list of meetings and projects at work and the long list of phone calls to return. I had gifts to buy and flights to schedule and oil to change and people to celebrate. But I wasn't seeing the people or the celebrations. I wasn't seeing anything beyond the chaos of my life and my home and my calendar.

We were hosting a baby shower, and I saw the shopping list and the favor ideas and the bookcases to be dusted, but underneath all those things, waiting for me like the red tree, was the real sight to behold. Waiting under the things to do was a story to be told.

For almost three years, Nate and Melissa have been wanting to have a child and have pursued all different roads, from medical procedures to international adoption. There have been many points on the journey that seemed like the end, because of paperwork, or money, or red tape. And then with just a few weeks' notice, Melissa was in the delivery room acting as a birth coach for the woman who chose them as adoptive parents for her baby girl, Selah Grace. That's what the shower was about. Not the favors or the food to be prepared or the things to be put away, but about the story of life and family and hope that it represented.

Hidden under the to-do list for the rehearsal dinner at our house is the story of my sister-in-law, Amy, whose wedding we were celebrating the next day. That night, over chicken korma and tandoori, two families told stories and laughed and prayed together, anticipating the next day's ceremony, anticipating the moment when the two families would become one. After a decade of broken, painful relationships, and the scars and heartbreak that go with them, Amy stood looking out over our city, surrounded by both families, as she married Austin, a man who is all of the things she hoped for, and all of the things that those men never were. Amy was a glowing bride, flushed with beauty and even more so with love. They say that some women acquire a new sense of beauty, that their lives take on a new bloom when they are deeply loved, and although my sensibilities prickle at the concept, when I see Amy now, I know that it's true. The day of her marriage to Austin began a new thing in her, a beautiful, lively, hopeful, generous way of living, a woman in full bloom. That's the luminous, beautiful thing hiding underneath the blur of the menu and the seating and the candles.

It looked like a full calendar, a whirl of events and to-do lists and grocery lists. But underneath it all, the month was a greatest hits album, a collection of stories, one after another, of the rich and gorgeous ways that God tells his stories through our lives. What looked like a shower or a dinner or one more night to clean up after was actually one of God's best gifts, worth celebrating, worth seeing. What looks like a plain old city street is just that until you lift up your eyes and see the red tree, and then you realize that this is no plain city street. This is a masterpiece just here for the week, our very own wonder of the world, and I just about missed it.

exodus

Last winter, I did a study on Exodus. Not the kind of Bible study I'm used to, because I usually do the kind where a bunch of friends meet at someone's house or a coffee shop and occasionally we do the actual study but mostly we talk and tell stories and pray at the end. This was the other kind, the kind where you have to have a really big commentary book, and it's hard to get through the reading if you're working on it during the commercial breaks of *The Bachelor in Paris* the night before. Not that I would ever do that, but if I had, you understand, it would have been quite challenging.

The other people in the study spoke Greek and Hebrew. I speak French, which is slightly less helpful in matters of theology, although much more helpful in fine dining and shopping. I feel good about the tradeoff, generally, but this study made me reconsider. The study took place at six in the morning, which is usually a time of day reserved for leaving for the airport, but only if I'm flying to a sunny place with umbrella drinks. Also, the study started in January. January in Grand Rapids is almost beyond description. It makes me think that maybe we heard wrong when God said hell is hot, because I think hell might be very,

very, mind-numbingly, scream-when-you-open-the-door cold, like January in Grand Rapids. Hot is tropical. Hot is flip-flops and the smell of coconuts, but cold is much more reminiscent of eternal punishment in my estimation. Like Grand Rapids in January.

So January. Grand Rapids. Six a.m. Exodus. Sounds like a party to me. I set my alarm and rode in my freezing cold car to the coffee shop in the black of night, ordered about a gallon of black coffee, and made my way to the church. About three weeks into the study, I found out I was pregnant, so throw that into the party mix. Fat, moody, and massively under-caffeinated. I sat at a long table, surrounded by people who, apparently, actually attended the Old Testament classes at their colleges, and several of whom even went back for a second helping at various seminaries.

What surprised me is that this time around, I found myself very connected to the story of Exodus. It's a great story, a big, sweeping story about the sea and the desert and the sky, but it's also a story of incredibly fine detail, like a Fabergé egg, like a large painting with teeny tiny brushstrokes. And as much as it's a very important story, about big themes and pervasive truths about the nature of God and his people, a finely wrought web of ideas and ideals, it's also about blood and bones and midwives and frogs and fires and bread.

Exodus, and the Bible as a whole for that matter, usually comes sanitized and shrink-wrapped, like chicken breasts at the grocery store in their flat, tidy little plastic packages. But when I read it this time, it seemed a lot more like a bunch of chickens in somebody's backyard, kicking up dust, squawking and screeching and pecking each other, with red and black and white feathers glinting in the hot sun. It's less like the commentary book, with its footnotes and indices, and more like a crime novel or a gothic tale of love and belief and betrayal, a story about family and fear and animals and anger.

Two of my favorite things are reading about food and watching TV about food. I drill my friends about what they order at restaurants and what they make for dinner. I bore my husband to tears with long descriptions of what I'm cooking for an upcoming dinner party and precisely what led me to each decision.

It might matter to me so much because I lived so far from that part of myself for so many years, eating fake diet food. I was so ashamed of my weight that I didn't let myself enter into the tactile, sense-oriented world of food, as a punishment and because I didn't trust myself. I guess I thought that if I let myself cook and touch and smell good food, I would start eating and not be able to stop. So I ate imitation food, like fat-free cheese and fat-free Cool Whip, and never let myself eat the kinds of food that you not only taste, but feel and smell and hear, like fresh mozzarella or flash-fried calamari, dusted in cornmeal, crackling and popping.

It might matter so much because feeding the people I love is a hands-on way of loving them. When you nourish and sustain someone, essentially, you're saying that you want them to thrive, to be happy and healthy and able to live well. It might matter to me because so much of the work I've done, both at church and as a writer, has taken place in my mind and in my heart, but not usually in my flesh and fingers. After a long day of writing or a long week of meetings, it returns me to myself to shop for food, to wander through the produce section, to wash and chop vegetables, to heat garlic and broth, to taste the sharpness of cheddar on whole grain bread.

Maybe it matters because even though so much of modern life and theology insists that what matters is my mind, my soul, my inner self, my heart, there is still this nagging part of me that knows on some deep level that the things we see and touch and hear and taste are spiritual, too. The dichotomy between spiritual and physical doesn't make sense to me now, because so much of God's work in my life has been the repairing and stitching together of the two. It didn't make sense to the Exodus writers either. The olives and the wine and the ideas and the stones and the mountain and the soul all matter deeply and signify something important, instead of the ideas and the souls being truly important, and the rest just being props on loan from the theater department.

Exodus brought to the surface and brought to life this little part inside me that whispered, "I thought so! I hoped so!" I think the best stories always do that, always resound somewhere below our stomachs with a sense of rightness, a sense of congruence with the way we were made and the way we understand ourselves.

On the mornings that we studied Exodus, I felt myself walk through the rest of the day differently. Some of it, of course, was that it felt like I had been awake since the dawn of time, which meant that by nine in the morning, I was ready for lunch, and by one in the afternoon, was more than ready to call it a day. But also I felt like my life, my actual daily, water and wine and blood and guts life, was a little ennobled, like I could stand up a little straighter. I ate my hummus and bread and olives at lunch feeling like I was a part of something old and elemental, like eating good food, fresh food made by someone's hands was something important. It made me think about the yarn of my scarf, and how someone made it with their hands, and how threads and garments and colors mattered so much when they built the ark of the covenant.

It made me feel like even though a million things are different in my life than they were then, like email and Gore-Tex and Zone Bars and dishwashers, some things are not so different, like bugs and yeast and the impulse to worship. There's still a big story, disguised as just regular life, and the big story is about love and death and God, and about bread and wine and olives, about forgiveness and hunger and freedom, about all the things we dream about, and all the things we handle and hold. Exodus was the Wild West, lawless and risky, and it's the cities we live in, bursting with life and meaning, and someday, when the future brings a world we can't even imagine now, Exodus will be there, in the songs and sounds and in the flesh and bones of a people who still wander and still yearn for home.

eggs and baskets

When I wrote a proposal for this book, it was January. The most natural thing in the world was to write a book on celebration, on the beauty and dimension of our everyday lives. Our previous year had been rich and busy and filled with great memories. We celebrated the thirtieth anniversary of my parents' church and went to Miami with our best friends and threw lots of great parties, celebrations for people we love. We went to Italy for the first time. My cousin Melody and my sister-in-law Amy both married wonderful men. For the first time in my life, I had really good hair.

When the book proposal was accepted, I drank a glass of fancy champagne with my best friend and felt so happy I could burst. Later that week, I found out I was pregnant, which made me feel guilty for drinking the champagne, but beyond thrilled.

Six weeks later, in the first blush of spring, just as I began sharing the news of our baby, I left my job at the church. It wasn't scandalous. I didn't steal from the offering plate, and there were no screaming matches or slamming doors. Looking back, I can see much more clearly what was happening, what had gone bad without my realizing it, what

I added to an already difficult situation. If I had been savvier and more aware, I would have resigned sooner. For a lot of reasons that I only understand now, I did the opposite: I tried and tried and tried to make something work that had stopped working a long time before I tried to salvage it. And I left, in the end, because I had no other choice.

More than a career setback, more than a professional disappointment, what it felt like to me was a heartbreak. I felt like something unraveled around me. I felt more vulnerable and powerless than I had in a decade. I didn't recognize myself in the mirror. One of my deepest secret beliefs is that I am actually not a good person at all, not a talented or helpful person in any way, and that someday everyone will find out even though I've managed to trick them for a little while, and this felt like the confirmation of all those feelings for all those years.

The point, I can see now, is not the job. The point is that the job was like a safety pin that was holding me together, and when the pin released, the whole system of my life and my self fell apart. People leave jobs all the time. I know. I know it's hard, and that it stings, and that you get over it and you move on and you find a new place to work. I know that jobs are things you do, that they're not badges of who you are, that they're not as important as your character or your family or your soul. I know.

I know those things, but something happened to me when I left my job. Something bad. I lost it, whatever *it* is. I lost that sense that I was okay, and that I would be okay again. I lost all belief in my future. I was sad and scared and ashamed. Without knowing it, without intending to, I had shoved way too much of myself into my job, more than a job can possibly bear, and I set myself up to fall a terrible distance if something were ever to happen to that job. And then, of course, it did. I put all my eggs in the job basket, until it became impossibly heavy, and it broke.

Another healthier, more deeply rooted person would have taken their healthy, rooted self to the next place. But I couldn't. When I gave back my computer and my keys, I gave back my identity, my confidence, my legitimacy. And it's not anyone's fault but my own. It's my fault for trying to find a shortcut, knowing full well that true spiritual depth and actual confidence have no substitutes.

After I stopped working, the first month was a blur. Some days were easy and some were hard, and I couldn't ever predict which ones would be which. I cried like Niagara Falls and wandered around my house reading novels and eating leftover Mexican food.

Sometimes I made myself go to church, but when I tried to sing, all that came out were tears, and when I tried to listen, my mind raced with scenarios: what could have been done, what could have been different, what could make it right, what magic words from what magic person would make it all go away. And then sometimes I stayed home from church. I had been working on Sundays for eight years. I had grown up in a pastor's home, where Sundays are game days. Since before we started dating, Aaron and I had been working together on Sundays. To stay home felt like a party being thrown without me. It felt cavernously lonely.

Because I was so ashamed and felt found out and embarrassed, I canceled things and didn't go to parties and didn't return phone calls and declined invitations for about six weeks. I talked with my husband and my parents and my housechurch, and almost no one else. After an exceedingly uncomfortable conversation with someone I ran into at my favorite breakfast restaurant, I mostly got takeout.

About two months after I left my job, I spoke at a conference. I was glad, conceptually, that I had a few speaking and consulting things on the calendar. I enjoy the work, and it helped me feel like I was earning some money for our family. But at the same time, I felt so deeply vulnerable. The last thing I wanted to do was stand up in front of anyone. What if someone asked me how things were going at my church? Did I have the right to say anything at all?

On the first morning of the event, I drove out to hear the other speakers. I didn't have to speak until the next day, but I wanted to go the first day to see what it was like. I had written my talk already—well, sort of.

On the way out there, I started feeling anxious, like I was going to get my blood drawn or going on a blind date. By the time I got to the parking lot, I was sobbing, so I stayed in the car to try to figure it out, and to try to fix my makeup. I was pregnant and tired, and the sky was deep blue, the sun slanting through the windshield. I slumped down in the driver's seat and laid my head back and cried.

I felt illegitimate. I felt like I had no right to speak at this conference anymore. My bio in the program had been printed when I was still working at the church, and now I felt like a liar, like a poser who was clinging to something that wasn't true anymore. I was unemployed and pregnant and the next day, I was going to have to stand up in front of almost a thousand people, and I had nothing to say to them. I cried and cried in the car, until I felt hollowed out and exhausted. I went in and stood at the back of the room for a few sessions, and then I went back home and rewrote every word of my talk.

The next morning, I was scheduled to speak after the producer of X-Men and before the man who engineered the Hummer. I swear. Actually X-Men. Actually the Hummer.

I walked out onto the stage and said, "I'm going to tell you right now that you are not going to like what I have to say. But I'm pregnant, which means I'm as big as a house, I eat like a linebacker, and I throw up in public. At this point, I have nothing left to lose. So I'm just going to tell you what I think."

And I did. I told them some of the things my friends and I had learned while we worked at churches. I told them the lessons we learned the hard way, and the things I wish I had known when I began. It wasn't clever or polished. There were no slides or video clips or touching anecdotes, but it was the best talk I have ever given, and I know exactly why. Because I had nothing left to lose, and it wasn't just because I was pregnant. I was a loser of the very worst kind, in my own mind, and I had given up on impressing them and figured that at the very least, I could give them a helpful thought for the car ride home. I didn't design a bestselling vehicle or produce a blockbuster movie, but I had spent almost a decade creating services in churches, and I told the truth as I see it about that work, about its value and its challenges.

And when the talk was over, I felt free. I didn't have a title or a business card anymore. I felt like I didn't have any ground to stand on, like I was in free fall. But what I found standing on that stage is that, to my great surprise, I had my stories, my own experiences and mistakes and successes, and that those are things you don't give back when you turn in your keys and your laptop. I had never felt more alone and vulnerable, walking out onto that stage, but when I walked off, I felt just exactly like myself. I didn't represent anyone or anything. I just took up my own space and told my own stories, stories that I earned along the way. And that was enough. I felt like, possibly for the very first time, I was holding my own eggs in my very own basket. And I hate how I got there, but it feels like an important place to be.

brothers, sisters, and barbecues

On the day I resigned from my job, our housechurch was having dinner at Joe's, whose apartment is the upstairs floor of an old house a few blocks north of our house. We walked up the wood staircase on the left, past his shoes lined up like soldiers. Aaron and I sat on the futon with our backs to the street, under the window. I was wearing my black-and-white striped Ella Moss shirt, because I knew it would be a hard day, and that shirt always makes me feel a little better.

We've been a housechurch for three years — Steve and Sarah, Annette and Andrew, Joe, Aaron and I. Annette and Andrew's baby son Spence has been a recent and wonderful addition, and we'll add another, our baby son, in the fall. The idea began as a weekly dinner and discussion and has woven itself into phone calls and vacations and borrowed lawnmowers and weekends at the lake and last-minute babysitting. Most of our families live out of town, and we've wormed our way into the family places in one another's lives, into the daily intimacies of homes and heartbreaks and hard conversations. We cry together and pray together and tell each other our secrets, and I think each one of us are surprised at what we've become in one another's lives.

During dinner, I told them what happened. I don't remember, really, what I told them, since it was so strange and fresh. I cried a little, but not as much as I would in the weeks to come. Annette's face, furthest away from me, was shocked and angry and protective. She was measured with her words, but I could see that she was upset, and that meant something to me. They asked questions and prayed for me at the end of the night, and in that house, in the dim light of Joe's laptop and stereo, I felt like I wasn't alone.

Two weeks later, we met at our house. I had been away for a long weekend at the beach with my family, and back to work for my last week, and was brimming over with anger and confusion and fear, wild with emotion. I made homemade macaroni and cheese and roasted vegetables, and after dinner, as we sat in the living room, they asked me how I was doing.

I was barely comprehensible, running from one fear to the next to the next, and I kept trying to change the subject, aware that I was out of control, and also that although this was the center of the universe to me, they must have been tired of hearing about it at that point. I felt embarrassed about not being able to move forward more quickly, and about being such a wreck, and about the tears that were all over my face and neck as I spoke. But every time I thanked them for listening and tried to turn the conversation, they turned it back and spoke to me like people who love me, because, I'm realizing, they are.

At one point, Joe, who generally listens without contesting, interrupted. I was rambling on and on about my fear and sadness, and he interrupted me. "You can feel however you want to feel right now. Except one thing. I keep hearing you say that you're embarrassed. I want you to stop saying that. You can feel angry, betrayed, whatever. But I don't think you have anything to be embarrassed about. And I'll never be embarrassed to be your friend."

I felt like I had been ground to dust, and those words started to put me back together. This is a story about a job, a church, a set of decisions and conversations and philosophies, but it is also a story about friendship. During a time when I had nothing to give but venom and tears, when I monopolized conversations and entertained the same conspiracy theories over and over again, this small circle of people were the words and fragrance and presence of God in unmistakable ways. I have never been so clingy and strange, so unmoored and lacking in appropriate small talk, and I am beyond thankful to my friends for sticking around in the worst of it.

When I see Steve or Joe or Andrew, my mind sometimes flashes back to my last staff meeting, when I was saying goodbye to a group of people I had worked with for years. Steve and Andrew and Joe stood in a half circle about an arm's length away from me, like bouncers or secret service. Both Steve and Joe are only children, but that day they became brothers to me.

In the days that followed, I wrote and cried, and my friends called a lot to check on me. Most days, I said I was going to write and instead read novels, devouring them like feasts, balancing a book on my pregnant belly, and lying to people when they asked if I was writing. Reading felt like escaping into other worlds, welcome departures from long, hollow days that I was supposed to be using to write a book about celebration. A book about celebration seemed like a bad cosmic joke, so instead of working on it, I read and read.

After about six weeks, there was a little something, a tentative shoot pushing up inside me, and I had a little tiny bit of energy and readiness to move forward. I thought about all sorts of ways to do that, and the best way I could figure out was to throw a party two months to the day of the date that I left my job. My therapist laughed and called it macabre, but I think I needed to know that even though a zillion things had changed, there were still a few things that hadn't. To be specific, I could still throw a really good party, people still love a good meal, and spring is still worth marking, after what seems like endless winter in Grand Rapids. I didn't tell anyone that that was the reason. I called it a "for no reason Monday night barbecue."

We filled our red wheelbarrow with ice and bottles of beer and soda, and we cooked steaks and set out cupcakes and frosting and sprinkles for the kids. I waddled my pregnant self around and chatted with a lot of the people I used to work with and missed terribly. We told stories and when the sun dipped down behind the backyard fence, I gathered up all our sweatshirts and fleeces and passed them out so we could stay out on the porch a little longer.

After everyone left, Aaron looked at me and said, "You're back." And I was, a little bit. And now I'm a fervent believer in the healing effects of a barbecue, because that one brought me back to life a little bit, macabre though it may have been.

It didn't change everything, but it moved me forward just an inch, and that inch might as well have been a marathon, because it made me smile and laugh and it made me feel like myself again, a newer self, but underneath the tears, still the same old me looking back at myself in the mirror. It felt like recovering something I thought might have been lost forever.

In the moments that I thought would be the loneliest, I didn't feel lonely. I had that little band of brothers and sisters everywhere I turned, calling me, emailing me, writing me letters, taking me out for breakfast, and sitting on the porch with me at our sad little barbecue, telling me the truth as they saw it, which was a lot more beautiful than the truth as I saw it then.

lent and television

I didn't grow up with a Lenten tradition, but in the last few years, I've started to celebrate it. One part of Lent is the decision to give up something, a practice or a way of living, in an effort to create space, to clean out a path for God's work in your life. Aaron and I stopped watching TV and movies for the six weeks of Lent. We knew it was the right thing for us, because we have somehow watched ourselves turn from thoughtful, creative, curious people to people who lay on the couch for hours on end, watching just one more episode of *The Jon Stewart Show* or the *Real World/Road Rules Challenge*. We're those people. We knew it would be good for us but also, like most things that are good for us, extremely painful.

Very unfortunately for me, I left my job right in the middle of Lent, and all the attending fear and sadness and anxiety and brokenheartedness landed with a thud in the newfound silence of our TV-free living room. To make matters much worse, I was pregnant, which meant, among other things, no drinking. I'm not a heavy drinker, but desperate times call for desperate measures, and if I had not been pregnant, the pain of that season might

have been eased by, say, ninety glasses of wine and an
E! True Hollywood Story marathon. But neither of those
were options, so I drank sparkling water and cried in the
cavernous, echoing silence.

In some moments it seemed cruel—why was this
happening to me when I had nothing to protect myself with?
Nothing to distract myself? Nothing to take me out of it even
for five seconds? I couldn't even take NyQuil in the night
when I was having the same imaginary conversation over and
over for hours. None of my tricks worked, and I was helpless
and exposed. I felt like I was in a winter storm with bare
legs and bare arms, nothing to buffer or protect me. I felt,
sometimes, like I had no skin, and everything struck bone
and vein directly.

It was excruciating, and it never let up, and although I
have not had this impulse before or since, I found that if I'm
being completely honest, I wanted to be self-destructive. I
wanted to make a mess. I wanted to stop the pain. I wanted
to act out physically what was boiling over inside me. And
the magic of pregnancy is that this little baby protected me
from myself. I couldn't bring myself to even think about doing
anything that would hurt the baby, so I couldn't do anything
less than healthy for myself. I wanted to starve myself,
drink ten martinis, take Ambien all day and all night, chain
smoke—something that would feel destructive and visceral,
something to match what was in my head, something to
give me a little reprieve from my broken heart. But instead I
waddled around and took my prenatal vitamins, and ate eggs
and cheese and drank cranberry juice, and between Lent and
pregnancy, I shuffled through that season clear-minded, wide
awake, unmedicated, unshielded.

What I believed at the outset that I needed from Lent
was space and silence, to create a space for God's voice and

presence in my life. And wouldn't you know it, just like he does, God bloomed into my quiet house and into my broken heart and into those forty-odd days like yeast in bread, leavening and changing everything. If I had known that my life would be sliced open so deeply, I would never have chosen the quiet that I committed to. But that's the magic of Lent, I think, that you sign yourself up for something, hoping maybe that God will slide something new into your life with him, and when he does, it's never what you thought, and never what would have been easy, and always just the right thing. What a gift, what graciousness, that silent season.

Lent is now over, but our house is still quiet. We had fantasies during Lent that as soon as the weeks passed, the TV would be on from morning until night, but at the same time, we knew that returning to our previous pattern would betray or dishonor Lent. So we've made ourselves a little plan, like the addicts that we are, and we turn it on sometimes, according to that plan, but largely, that scary terrible silence is here to stay. Every once in a while, I even have moments where the silence keeps me company, feels comforting. We're making peace, I guess, the silence and I.

a funeral and a wedding

for the Spencer family

Early on a Tuesday morning in May, just before Memorial Day weekend, my brother called me. I missed his call, and I knew by how early it was that something must be wrong, so I called back over and over until he picked up. When I finally got him, I was on the corner of Madison and 28ᵗʰ Street, by the BP station, and the rising sun blurred my vision as I waited to turn right.

Our friend Clark had been in an accident the night before, he told me, and he had been killed. I was on my way to the church but kept going past it, to South Haven, where Clark lived, where my mom was, where Todd was going to meet us. We sat silently in our friend Jodi's house, waiting for Todd, drinking coffee, and when he drove up and got out of the truck, he hugged me so hard and for so long that I thought he might knock me down, that I might bend under the weight of his grief. For the next several days, we told stories and cried and cried.

The whole town stopped, because Clark was an extraordinary person, the fourth of five boys in an extraordinary family. In the evenings of that week, we went over to his family's house, and two of Clark's friends played their guitars and sang, and we listened and sang along and leaned on one another, and in the silences every few minutes someone would murmur, "Clark would have loved this." And he would have. They sang Damien Rice's "Volcano," and now when I listen to that song in my car, I cry and think about Clark.

He was twenty-one. He painted our dining room bright turquoise with my brother when we moved to Grand Rapids, and he sometimes sat with me at the Sunday night service at church and helped me make dinner afterward. Last Christmas, my mom was in a terrible car accident, and none of us could get to her, but Clark did, and he picked her up and made sure she got back home safe. We called him my mom's angel, and it feels doubly cruel that when her car crashed, he was there to help, but when his car crashed, no one could help him.

On the day of the visitation, literally every flower in town was at the funeral home. The florists had no more flowers, and that felt fitting, that every fragile, beautiful living thing in town wanted to be where Clark was.

Clark's funeral was on a Friday, a cool blue-skied Friday, and straight from the funeral, I flew to Chicago, because one of my oldest and dearest friends was getting married and asked me to officiate the ceremony. I had to leave straight from Clark's funeral to go to her rehearsal and rehearsal dinner. On a small plane over the lake, alone except for the pilot, I felt brittle and hollowed out, like I had cried out all of my blood that week. I felt the two events gain clarity from one another, and I was strikingly aware of the connections between them.

Clark was loved deeply and expressively by his parents and his four brothers, who stroked his hair and touched his lifeless fingers throughout the visitation. In the small church, seven or eight hundred people packed into a room for about a hundred and fifty. My brother loved Clark, and their friendship was one of the closest Todd had ever experienced. Clark was supposed to move into Todd's new house and had just sold his own house the day before the accident.

As I flew over the lake and joined Brannon and Chris and their families for the rehearsal and dinner, I felt urgent and purposed. I wanted to whisper to them, hold them by the shoulders. I wanted to say, "This is a good thing that you're doing, making a new family, joining together in love, promising to walk through life together. Because I saw something this week that I pray you will never experience, but if you do, may God bless you with a family like Clark's family. May God give you brothers to stand with, or a wife's hand to hold, or a sister to weep with, because we won't make it through these things alone. We can't stand in the way of death, but when it comes, we can stand in its face together, and celebrate life and celebrate family and celebrate having loved fiercely and expressively."

Standing in front of Chris and Brannon, during their wedding ceremony at the horse farm where Brannon had been riding all her life, I looked at her four sisters and his best friends and both of their parents, and I invited them all to celebrate this new family, because a new family makes the world better. It brings people together, creates new connections, creates bonds that we all need in daily ways, and then desperately, when death comes to our home the way it did to Clark's home.

Brannon was an impossibly beautiful bride, and Chris a handsome groom, and the light came through the trees in the most perfect way. It felt like a deep honor to pronounce them husband and wife, a hopeful and delicate moment rising from a week of despair.

As they danced that night, with such happiness and abandon and sweetness, I sat at the edge of the dance floor with my brother, and we both knew that the other was thinking of Clark, and who Clark might have married, and what Todd's wedding day will be like without Clark standing with him, and I thought I might burst at that moment, so full of sadness and beauty, so thrilled for this new family, this new symbol of possibility and life, and so heavy with the grief I carried with me. And that moment felt like a rare gift, like the essence of life and love and family was sitting in my hand, like a tiny bird.

mothers and sons

My mom and I spent a week in Chicago this summer taking a class at a Catholic graduate school in the city. It was hot and windy, and the class was long. I was pregnant, and we were both exhausted. Every day, when the class was finished, we went straight back to the hotel and laid on our beds trying to decide whether or not to go back the next day. It took all of our energy to decide on dinner and walk to a restaurant, so several nights we opted for takeout so we could sit on our beds eating Japanese noodles and flatbread.

On Tuesday morning of that week, while we ate pancakes at a restaurant by our hotel, my dad called from South Haven to tell us that my brother had been in a bad car accident. I could see my mom's face but couldn't hear my dad's words. When I heard her ask, "How bad is he?" I felt sick, like the lights in the restaurant were too bright and too hot or like I had swallowed a big piece of my plate thinking it was pancake. I wanted to scream at the man beside us yammering away about the window replacement business. My mom gave me the quick thumbs-up that he was fine, while she nodded, listening to Dad on the other end of the phone, but I still wanted the window man to shut it, so I could concentrate. Todd called a few minutes later to tell us that he was fine, and we felt blessed and lucky and a little bit like it wasn't real, because he sounded so fine on the phone.

After our class, though, back at the hotel, we talked to Dad again, and he told us a little more clearly how bad the accident had been, and how different it would have been if the cars had been a second earlier or later in the intersection. We started to understand that it was more than a lucky break, and that he could have died that morning, and that this was not a near miss but a miracle. We tried not to think about Clark's accident, in the same town, on an early summer morning just like that one. My mom and I sat on our beds in our hotel room, far from Dad and Todd and Aaron. It was a Tuesday night, and on Thursday, Todd was turning twenty-seven.

All at once, my mom began to cry. She cried and cried for her son, for what could have happened, for being far away from him. She came and sat next to me on my bed, and we both put our hands on my belly, on my son, while she talked to him through her tears.

She said, "Be careful, Henry. Be careful. We love you so much. We love you." We sat there for a long time, she thinking about her big, grown son, and me thinking about my tiny, curled up inside me. I realized in that moment how terrifying it is to be a parent, that someday, a few days before Henry's twenty-seventh birthday, someone could run a red light early in the morning, and there will be nothing in the world that I can do about it. That thought makes me unable to breathe.

I know, cognitively, that all of parenting is an effort to give your kids the ability to live without you, beyond you. I know that Henry will make me mad, and probably date girls who wear too much makeup, or he'll have bad table manners to spite me, or choose to play dangerous sports. I know he will break my heart into slivers over and over as he grows away from me, and that he should grow away from me, that that's the only right thing for him to do.

But that night, on that bed, feeling so far away from my brother, my mother's son, sitting together with her, with our hands on my tiny son in my belly, I felt one of the first splitting aches that must be motherhood. I felt in that moment that nothing in the world could hurt my son, that I am superhuman in my love for him, that if he needed me, I would fly or bend steel or wrinkle time with the force of my love. And in the same moment, I knew that all mothers feel that way, and that all mothers also feel the exact inverse, the terrifying awareness that people run red lights, and that we won't be there to stand in front of our son's cars, shielding them from danger with our superhuman selves.

I felt powerful and powerless in the same instant, full of rabid, crushing love, and also small and out of control and scared for all the life that my son will have to live without my protection. Parenting for me feels like a love so big I can't manage it, a force so visceral I can't contain it.

I know that when Henry is born, I will change his diapers and feed him and keep him clean and warm. Those are the physical things I can do for him. But what I want to do for him takes my breath away. I want to twist and remake the world around his little self, to shine it up and rearrange it and make it great and special for him. I want to walk ahead of him, making sure things are safe, and walk behind him, keeping an eye on him. I want every day of his life to be happy, and I feel like I could move the sun with the intensity I feel. I knew that a baby would be vulnerable and would need my protection, physically and otherwise. But what I know now as I watch my mother is that it doesn't matter how big a son gets, a mother always feels, however illogically, that she should have been there to save him from whatever it was that hurt him.

My mother weighs a hundred pounds, and my brother is a man now, six-two and strong. But that night I saw the size of her love for him, bigger than the ocean, beyond words and logic and sense. And I feel it, too, for my son, like a sickness or falling in love or falling down the stairs, its inevitability and its enormity.

the cat's pajamas

Last week Grandpa Niequist, my husband's grandpa, had a heart attack. When Aaron got the call from his mom, he came to look for me at the coffee shop where I was writing. We got tea, sat at the corner table, and cried. I've only seen him cry maybe ten times in our life together. We sat together on that gray, cold day, and talked about Grandpa and cried. Aaron's eyes become very green when he cries. We sat, waiting for a phone call, waiting for an update.

I had a doctor's appointment that day. Henry's heartbeat inside me was strong and fast, and the juxtaposition of life and death, of Grandpa's body pulling him toward death and Henry's body wiggling inside me, bursting with life, made my heart heavy and thankful and sad.

In the midst of those two things, my dad was at the hospital for tests. He is fifty-five and generally very healthy, but has been sick for two months with a strange litany of things, and now they're doing more CT scans, more blood work. They'll have the results later this week.

I tried to work but couldn't. I felt far away from all of these men in my life, far from Grandpa in a hospital bed, and my dad awaiting test results, and Aaron, at work, pretending he hadn't been crying, and Henry, who is with me in the deepest sense, but whose face I can't yet see, whose tears I can't yet wipe. And I felt powerless against the body and time and medicine, and I wished that the sheer force of my love could reverse it all, and I wished that I could be ten places at once, and that if I was, it would matter. A knot of anxiety twisted like a knife, around and around and around, and in that moment the world seemed so fragile and life so dangerous and risky, and more than I could hold inside my heart and my mind. I sat at my desk, fingers on the keyboard ready, but my mind was running too fast to land, and I felt like things were breaking and turning to dust before my eyes, like the earth was shifting and out of control. I stared at a blank screen.

Aaron's mom called again later that week to tell us that Grandpa was gone. He died surrounded by his family, telling stories and singing to him. He was two months shy of his eightieth birthday.

One of the particular needles of sadness is that he will not meet our son, who will be born next month. Henry would have been Grandpa's first great-grandchild, a fact that brought him much joy. When we talked with him about the baby, he would shake his head proudly, and say, "Another generation of Niequists." We were looking forward to a picture at Thanksgiving, of Grandpa, Dan, Aaron, and Henry, four generations of Niequist men. It is strikingly sad to come so close to that, and to know that picture will never be taken, will never be framed on a mantel or tucked away in an album.

When I first met Grandpa, he took Aaron and me fishing in the Florida Keys. We left early in the morning, with sandwiches that Grandma packed for us. Grandpa took us out to his best fishing hole, near the bridge over to the next key, and we cast out into the bright water over and over for hours. Grandpa took my fish off the hook for me, but he made me reach into the bucket myself to grab a live shrimp for bait, even though it took me several tries each time, and even though I yelped every time I plunged my hand into all the squirmy, wriggling shrimp. He loved that I was a boater, that I could tie a decent knot and knew port from starboard. At the end of the day, he told Aaron that he thought I was the cat's pajamas.

When we received the phone call, we went back to Chicago for the weekend and spent hours and hours talking about Grandpa, about his life, and about what it was like to be a part of his family. Yesterday at the funeral, at end of the eulogy, which was beautiful and was the story of a life very well lived, the pastor talked about Grandpa's love for his family, and his sons told stories about fishing trips and family holidays and memories of the house he built for his young family and lived in until he died.

The day of his heart attack, Grandpa was trimming trees with a chainsaw. My father-in-law always said that Grandpa would die with his boots on, and I know that he meant it figuratively, but it happened literally. Grandpa spent his last wakeful moments working in the backyard near the pond where he taught his children and grandchildren to swim.

Each of us who knew him well have story after story of ways that he loved us and made us feel important, and we interrupted each other on the day of his funeral, fighting to tell all the stories of our life together, our life with Grandpa. His life had an epic quality to it; a quintessentially American sense; a nostalgic, charmed quality; a story of family and music and Sundays in the backyard pond with the grandkids.

If you were to ask his children and grandchildren about him, they would tell you the things he taught them—

that family comes before business, that hard work matters, that faith is the most important thing. They would not tell you he was perfect, but they would tell you that because of him, because of his role in each of their lives, they are better people, better fathers and mothers, better husbands and wives, better doctors and business owners, better church members, and better followers of Jesus.

We left the funeral tired and sad, but proud—proud to have been his children and grandchildren, proud to have been bit players in such an extraordinary story.

So goodbye, Grandpa Niequist. You're the cat's pajamas.

pennies

I collect champagne flutes, because I love to celebrate, and I collect pennies. I started doing it in college, right around the time that people kind of stopped using them. That bothered me, I guess, so now I keep pennies. And like with anything you're looking for, or anything you collect, the more aware you are of them, the more you see.

It's like when you're engaged, or, even worse, about to be engaged, and your ability to spot diamonds is sharper than a jewel thief's. You can be walking through a restaurant and get to your table and say, "Honey, on our way in, I saw an emerald cut, about three quarters of a carat, a princess, and a cushion cut, and our server's ring is platinum, not white gold." And your boyfriend is like, "Mmmmm. Do I smell wings?"

I started to see pennies everywhere—in the backs of drawers, under the couch cushions, at the sticky bottom of the center console of cars. There are always a few, along with bobby pins and ticket stubs, in the purses that aren't used every day. You find them when you need that particular purse for a particular occasion. And then you move them to some other random place. They collect, of their own accord, it seems, on windowsills and in jacket pockets and on kitchen counters.

Before I started collecting pennies, I used to throw them away, along with gum wrappers and used Kleenex. No one accepts them anymore, really. I keep hearing that they're going to take them out of circulation. Bank tellers glare at me when I try to hand them several hundred and ask for dollars and quarters instead. The man at the Mexican restaurant where I eat doesn't want them. I get the same thing every time. It always comes to $6.04. Six-oh-four. I hand him six or a ten or a twenty and then dig in my pockets for the pennies, but he shakes his head. No pennies, no.

I went through a toll booth once and paid the whole thirty-five cents with pennies. My friend and I giggled as I threw them in the basket one by one (plink plink plink) and the cars behind me honked. When I worked at a little surf shop in junior high, at the end of the day, we would balance the register to the cent, to the penny. But no one does that anymore.

All of a sudden, the loss of these pennies seemed tragic to me. So I started collecting them, in a pale blue bowl that my cousin Georgia gave me for Christmas. I sort them out of the more substantial silver coins in my pocket and set them in their new place, the smooth blue bowl. I don't know what I will do with them, but there is something satisfying about watching their numbers grow, a little army of copper coins. It soothes me to think that if there is a place for them, then there is a place for everything. It seems immeasurably mature of me to do this, like having dish towels and stamps and spare light bulbs all in their respective places. It feels to me that if these worthless little coins have a place, then they have a meaning. And then if I have a place, I have meaning.

In a world where less and less actually exists, where you can spend money without actually having any in your hand, and you can chat in a room without actually chatting or being in that room, these smooth copper pennies are rare, curious things. They are the real thing.

So now I'm amassing pennies like you wouldn't believe. Maybe someday I will melt them all down and make a trophy. Maybe I will grout them into my bathroom tile. Maybe I will shellac them in tidy rows onto my kitchen cabinets or make jewelry with them. I don't know yet. But when I walk by the blue bowl in the kitchen, I find myself absently running my fingers through the coins, sure for the moment that there are things that are real and understandable, and therefore good, things I can hold on to when my hands feel empty.

My friend goes to a spiritual director, and I was asking her about it, and she said, basically, Sister Carmen asks her to talk about her life, and she points out the presence and action and grace of God when my friend didn't even notice it was there. So it was there all along, and the trick is learning to see it.

Each one of our lives is shot through, threaded in and out with God's provision, his grace, his protection, but on the average day, we notice it about as much as we really notice gravity or the hole in the ozone. So what I'm trying to do is learn to see the way Sister Carmen sees. Because once you start seeing the faithfulness and the hope, you see it everywhere, like pennies. And little by little, here and there, you realize that all of life is littered with bright copper coins, that all of life is woven with bits and stories of God's goodness.

When I look back now, with these new eyes, it's like there's a bright copper path I was walking on and didn't even know it. And it's the handful of pennies that I'm clutching in my sweaty hand that gives me the faith and the strength to move forward. What gives me hope is the belief that God will be faithful, because he has been faithful before, to me and the people around me. I need the reminders. I need to be told that he was faithful then, and then, and then. Just because I have forgotten how to see doesn't mean it isn't there. His goodness is there. His promises have been kept. All I need to do is see.

So when I'm on the edge, peering over into the unknown, trembling and terrified to move forward, devastatingly afraid to take that next step, I practice believing that full life is beyond the fear. I know that God's voice has led me to this exact place, and I grab a few pennies. They are sacred reminders that God is God, that he is leading my life, and that he is saying to me, as he has been saying to his people throughout history, I will never leave you, and I've left reminders all around, if you have the eyes to see them.

When my husband was small, and he went to visit his grandparents in Milwaukee, Grandpa always took them down to walk by the creek and told them to look for something shining in the water, because you never know, there could be coins in the river. So they would look and look and look, and wouldn't you know it? Every time, they would find quarters and pennies and dimes, and they would go home and show Grandma, who was always surprised and excited for them.

At Grandpa's funeral, we were all telling stories about Grandpa, and one of the cousins remarked that it took her *years* to figure out that Grandpa was walking just ahead of them, throwing handfuls of change into the creek.

My husband stared at her. He had never known that, until the day of the funeral. Looking back, he says, he should have known, because sometimes there were even brand new toys and baseball mitts floating in this little creek, alongside the bright copper coins.

III

hide and seek

About 90 percent of the reason I write is for what it does on the inside of my life, and about 10 percent for what it produces on paper. Three years ago, a friend of mine invited me to do a writing project with him. I said yes because I studied literature in college and because I love to read. I had been writing the occasional essay and some text for different video projects and songs we had been working on at church. So I started tapping away, feeling pretty sure that it would not be so hard, really.

It was an unmitigated disaster. Not because the writing was bad. But because there simply was no writing. None. I made lots of excuses, a few legitimate. I was starting a new job at the church, and jobs at churches are demanding and very draining and have irregular hours. All true. I started to feel a low-grade anxiety and guilt all the time, like a hum, but instead of looking for the source of the hum, I just avoided my friend who was doing the project with me and found more and more ways to distract myself. Summer wasn't a good time for me, nor were the holidays, nor were weekdays, because of work, or weekends. I canceled meetings with my friend, missed deadlines, cried, made excuses, complained about my lot in life, pitched crazy ideas that involved me not actually having to do any of the writing, and cried some more.

For me, writing is about control. Or, more accurately, loss of control. Maybe you are a writer, and you disagree because writing for you feels more like walking on the beach or getting a massage. Well, maybe you and I should never meet for coffee. Writing for me feels like getting naked in public. It feels like falling to the bottom of a well and finding lots of creepy crawly things down there with you. It feels like opening up a box of snakes. It feels kooky and scary and out of control. It makes me upset sometimes, because it makes me honest. When I sit down to write, for awhile I read magazines and send emails and wander around, and then when I finally get up the guts to crack through the ice of my mind, I find myself in an odd universe of feelings I didn't know I felt, and memories I didn't know I carried. After I've been writing for a while, I get sort of sensitive and strange, like a theater kid in high school.

I have a condition my husband and I call "crazy brain." It's like being hyperactive in your brain instead of your body. For the record, I am so not hyperactive in my body. I could sit on the couch for the better part of a decade if someone were bringing me snacks and novels. But in my brain, it's like there's a hamster wheel, and it gets running so fast that I find myself rubbing my forehead to settle things down in there. It usually starts out first thing in the morning, before the alarm, with something pretty small like what I should have for breakfast. And then I think about how I want to go to the Real Food Café, which is my favorite, and how I would like scrambled eggs, English muffin toast, sliced tomatoes, cream cheese, and coffee. Then I think about how we shouldn't eat out so much, because we're just spending massive amounts of money on things I should be cooking for us at home. Then I think about all the other things that we spend our money on, but shouldn't, like TiVo and witty T-shirts from Urban Outfitters, and I start to fear that our children will live in a hovel because Mommy and Daddy spent all their disposable income on eggs and T-shirts, and with all that money, we should have done some home improvements, or at least gone to Europe, instead of frittering it all away on takeout. And then I think about how unsafe our house is for babies, and all the things we should do to baby-proof it. Then I think about moving, which makes me anxious because showing a house is so horrific and you have to keep it so clean. If I'm going to keep my house that clean, I might as well live in it for a while. Which makes me think about our future. Am I listening closely enough for where we should be going with our lives? What if I've missed the cosmic bus to my best future because I was watching E!? What if, fundamentally, I'm not deserving of a good future, because I am systematically wasting my life, and God has given up on me once and for all, because I am so bad at life and can never remember everything on my grocery list, and I don't tweeze my eyebrows often enough, and I wear pajamas to the coffee shop and am not really contributing on any large scale to the world becoming a better place, because, frankly, who in their right mind would let me, with all of my problems?

That's the hamster wheel. And writing is when I let the hamster off the wheel and let it run loose for a while, wherever it wants, sniffing around. When I write, I believe the risky thought that all the ideas might have a place, instead of just running themselves around and around in a circle. Writing gives me a place to use all the flashes and thoughts and rabbit trails that rattle around in my head making me crazy. Writing is my best chance at happiness, and it is the riskiest thing I can do. But that's how life is. The riskiest things always yield the best, most beautiful things.

One of the true hazards in writing is that you yearn to write deeply honest things that rise up from lessons learned the hard way ... and then you have to learn those lessons the hard way. I had written a chapter on jealousy, and after I looked at it for a while, it seemed sort of flat and cartoony. I prayed for a new way to write that chapter, an incisive and honest way to talk about being jealous. And not a week later, wouldn't you know it, at dinner with some friends, I found out something about a mutual friend of ours that absolutely annihilated me with jealousy. It was a thousand straws that broke a thousand camels' backs, and I was tumbling around and around with these vicious, terrible jealous feelings, like I was in the spin cycle with a box of rocks. That's the last time I pray for a good chapter on anything, except being gorgeous or winning the lottery or something. You pray for wonderful, honest, gritty, tender stories to write, but then you have to live through them.

What writing teaches me, over and over, is that God is waiting to be found everywhere, in the darkest corners of our lives, the dead ends and bad neighborhoods we wake up in, and in the simplest, lightest, most singular and luminous moments. He's hiding, like a child, in quite obvious and visible places, because he wants to be found. The miracle is that he dwells in both. I knew he dwelt in the latter, the bright and beautiful, because I had been finding him there for years, in the small moments of beauty and hope that poke through the darkness of our days.

But lately I have been finding him not just under the darkness, but in it, right within the blackness and deadness of these days. I have found a strange beauty in the darkness, one I've never seen, a slower, subtler beauty, like how an old woman's skin is more telling and rich than a teenage girl's, how a storm can make you feel more deep emotion than a sunny day ever did. When I write, I find a whole new universe I never saw before, like being underwater for the first time, having never before seen what's under the glassy surface.

Sometimes when I'm writing, if I try really hard, I can move more slowly, like a dancer or a mime, and taste things more vividly, and see not just the trees and the grass, but the individual leaves and blades. Things are richer and brighter than I thought, now that I have slowed down enough to see them. I can see that for years I have been wanting to live this way, and at the same time have been very afraid of what I'd have to give up for it. And in some ways, I have given up everything, but at the same time, nothing essential is missing. Everything was lost, and even more has been recovered, like things that are carried out to sea and then wash up on the same beach, alongside entirely new and glimmering treasures.

Every life tells a story, through words and actions and choices, through our homes and our children, through our clothes and dishes and perfume. We each play a character in a grand drama, and every stage direction matters. We tell our stories, and we let God's story be told through our stories. We hide and we seek, and we lose ourselves in the best possible way, and find things around us and inside ourselves that we never expected. We tell God's story as we live and discover our own. We know that God is a storyteller. He's a mad scientist and a father and a magician, and certainly, he's a storyteller. And I don't know if there's anything better in the world than when we lay ourselves wide open and let his story become our story, when we screw up our fists and our courage and start to tell the truest, best stories we know, which are always God's stories.

broken bottles

Four years ago, I went to Africa with my mother and my brother and a friend of ours, who is the president of a relief agency. We went to Kenya, Uganda, and Zambia, and it freaked me out. It unnerved and unraveled me, and seeped into my dreams and my thoughts the way a particularly evocative movie or song does. Africa is nothing if not evocative. It's a place of such unimaginable beauty and dignity and expanse and possibility, and such unfathomable suffering and despair and disease and decay. It is at once so alive and so wracked by death, so powerful in its landscape and physicality, and so powerless under the weight of famine and political upheaval and disease. Its intensity scared me and overwhelmed me, and I feel like I wandered through many long days there, stunned and tired and unable to digest what I saw and heard, and more specifically, what I felt inside myself. And even now, four years later, I'm still piecing together what happened in me and what was happening around me in those cities and villages.

I wasn't ready for Africa. I had been to lots of other places, but I wasn't ready for the chaotic jumble of people and homes and music and muddy winding paths through the shanty-towns in Nairobi or the huts in the Ugandan bush, tiny huts in the middle of a blinding, parched expanse that went on as far as I could see. I wasn't ready for the hospitals in Zambia, where I cried and hid my eyes as much as possible, where the smell of death and the cries of people in extreme pain rang out over row after row of rusted beds with dirty and bloodied sheets.

In the most disorienting change of venue, I flew from Zambia, through Frankfurt, back to O'Hare, and on to the Caribbean for a family vacation. I wish I could say that I wasn't seduced by the the smooth deck and bright white sails of the boat we stayed on, that I couldn't swim in the perfectly warm navy-blue water because I was so overcome by the horror of what I had seen. I'm ashamed to say that wasn't the case, and even more ashamed to say that I was glad to be there, glad to no longer be in Africa. I almost tried to let the warm salty water and the soothing wind wash away the smells and sounds of Africa.

I wanted away, out from under what I had seen and felt. I talked about it a little bit, but it was so hard to explain, and so hard to go back into those places inside me. I didn't know how to tell my husband or my friends that Africa had done something bad inside me, had demonstrated to me a part of myself I didn't know I had. For one of the first times in my life, my beliefs and perspectives bowed and flattened under the weight of my experience. Before I went there, I wanted to invest myself in the healing, in some small way, of Africa. But when I was there, I just wanted to leave, and I was ashamed and surprised by that part of myself.

I wanted to shut my eyes and stop seeing the images of starving children. I wanted to sleep at night without smelling the scent of smoke from open fires and the sounds of guards' heavy footsteps outside our doors. Everyone I know, it seems, wants to go to Africa, wants to volunteer for a few days in an AIDS clinic or an orphanage. And that's good. It's a good impulse to want to see it with your own eyes and to want to be a part of the solution. I encourage them to go and recommend organizations and churches to connect with, but inside myself, I whisper to them, *Be careful.* You will be haunted by what you find there, and you won't be able to wash away what you've seen and heard. You will see things and hear things, and then you will be responsible for them, for telling the truth about who you are and who you discover you are not, and for finding a way to make it right.

I had to make things right in two ways. I had to do something personally to make things right in Africa, because now I knew too much and couldn't erase the images and sounds that had embedded themselves in me, like seeds planted in a garden. I had to make something right there, which is both enormously daunting and shockingly simple. Daunting because of how massive and tangled the roots of the issues have become — it is about famine and sexual violence and patriarchy and racism and economics and medicine, and when you think you've knitted together the magical solution, one pull on one string unravels the whole thing and leaves you with a mountain of new questions, while the clock ticks away lives by the dozen. And then again, shockingly simple, because there are such good, smart people doing such courageous, good, smart things, and what can be done with tiny little bits of money is just dazzling.

Also, though, and more difficult, I had to make things right within me. I had to confront the person I found on that trip, the one who wanted to fly home the first night and pretend the whole thing was not real. That's the trick, I think. That's why actually getting on a plane and going there is dangerous and very important. Because I could not forget about it, as desperately as I wanted to. I had to clear away space in my mind and my heart, spaces previously occupied by easy things—groceries to buy, albums to download, people to call—and replace them with the weight of Africa, a heavy, dark thing to carry with me, something under which to labor, something under which to tremble. Because once you see it, you will never be able to un-see it, and once you see it, you will be responsible for it, and for the self it reveals back to you.

Somehow on that trip, I grew softer and harder in unexpected places. But more than that, I've grown since that trip, because there is a new thing inside me, however thoroughly I tried to escape it. Africa has grown like a stubborn stalk in the soil of my life, despite my resistance, despite my fear and selfishness.

It took some time, after the trip. It took some time for me to want to talk about Africa, to want to read about it again, to want to hear about it at church. But I saw it, and carried it with me, and despite my best efforts, couldn't un-see it, so all I could do, it seemed, was enter back in, in an entirely new way. I will never recapture my naïveté, my idealism about what magical solution might just bind up all the broken pieces. But I practice listening, learning, and praying. I practice telling the truth about myself, the truth I was too proud to admit four years ago, that I'm scared and that when faced with death, I cried, instead of rising up like a nurse or a prophet. I hid my eyes. But I don't anymore.

The baby growing in my belly as I write has brought my memories of that trip into focus. What was distant and abstract is now bursting into my field of vision in sharp relief: mothers could not feed their babies. I understand that now in a way that I did not, could not, then. My own mother has said that AIDS in Africa will be addressed and eventually healed by mothers. Then, I thought she meant women in general, possible mothers, I guess. But the non-mother-me who took that trip didn't get something that the mother-me does now. Everything looks different—Africa and my own neighborhood and my own belly and the pregnant bellies I saw there, mothers carrying babies who will be born hungry and live hungry every day of their lives.

There is a food truck that comes to our neighborhood twice a month. A wonderful local church sets up the truck in their parking lot, and people line up around the block for potatoes and formula and apples. Our housechurch volunteers sometimes, unpacking the food and packing it into the laundry baskets and bags and buckets that our neighbors bring. I'm silenced every time, watching women just like me, carrying babies they love the way I love mine, tucking onions and corn and juice into baskets, because without the food truck, they would not have enough food for their children.

What happened in me on the other side of the world is working its way through my life like yeast through dough, right in my neighborhood. I help feed people on Thursday afternoons, a tiny thing, but one that is important to me, because once you see something, you can't un-see it. I saw the women in that line with their babies, and I can't un-see them. And I don't want to.

One night in Africa we climbed to the highest point we could find, through waist-high bushes and bramble and thorny underbrush, and when we came to the top, we looked out at the sun setting across a majestic and regal land, land that had been given and taken and stolen and drenched with blood, but land that at that moment was glowing with the softness of the fading sun and the rich purples and greens of harvest time. The property on which we stood was walled on all sides, and the top of the wall was spiked with broken bottles so that no one could scale it without being cut on the glass. We stood inside the wall, and the broken bottles glinted in the sun like sparklers, keeping people in, keeping people out, twinkling and beautiful, and at the same time, embedded with violence and division, and in those two things, those twin natures, lies Africa.

And in Africa I discovered my own twin natures, extending to me two hands, one holding terror and despair and one hope, and day by day, I make my choice. There is hope for Africa, and there is hope for me, and for my neighborhood, for the shards of broken bottles that puncture and divide us all.

prayer and yoga

Prayer, to me, is sort of like yoga, on several levels. It's good for me and helps me, and to be quite honest, I say I do it way more than I actually do. When someone asks, "Do you do yoga?" I answer, "Absolutely. I love it. It totally makes me feel better."

What I mean, in the strictest sense, is that every week I intend to go to yoga three times and I occasionally make it to one class, and I have several pairs of yoga pants, and some yoga DVDs and flashcards, and every once in a while, if I'm really feeling bad, I do a few sun salutations before bed. So really, I'm yoga-ish.

Prayer, in my life, is similar. If you ask me about prayer, I have the books, the journals, a few transcendent experiences to report from the last decade, lots of good reasons why every person should do it, and not a ton of extremely current experiences rushing to mind. I believe in it, conceptually. I feel better when I do it. I believe my life would be better if I did it a lot, like yoga, but when it comes right down to it, I'm prayer-ish.

But something has to get you back to yoga, and something has to get you back to prayer, and in my experience, the surest thing in either case is desperation. I wait until my life has become so completely unlivable and the person I am has become so deeply unmoored from reality and hope and goodness, that I break down and pray.

Today I am desperate enough to pray. When I think about prayer, about what it is and what it brings to my life and what it tells me about the way life is, I realize, for the thousandth time, that the alternative is about as smart as building your house on marshmallow fluff or taking Flintstone vitamins to cure cancer.

Unfortunately, though, most of the time what I believe in instead of prayer is my own patched-together sense of how life ought to work. In my system, people who work hard end up okay. Also, people who are smart and careful and keep the batteries in their smoke alarms up to date will be safe. People who order their toast dry and only smoke on very special occasions will be healthy. And so on. This personal worldview has actually functioned reasonably well. I get my oil changed, I fill out my jury duty questionnaire, and I expect that life will continue to be kind to me, because of my good citizenship and car maintenance, because I am living up to my end of the bargain.

I don't tell anyone about this worldview. I tell them, you know, God is in control, and we never know where that path leads, and a man plans his way but God knows his steps, and I lean not on my own understanding. But secretly, I do absolutely lean on my own understanding. I do it so that I don't feel so out of control and blind to the world, so that I can have a plan and manage my life and not feel like something's coming around the corner that I can't predict and don't have insurance for. I believe in my own ability to figure out my life, and top-secretly, I don't want it to be all misty and mysterious. I don't want to say that the future is in

God's hands and could go any way he chooses. That sounds terrifying to me. I want guarantees. I want the future in my hands. I want healthy, intelligent children who never sneer at me or wear slutty clothes or play violent video games. I want a nice bathtub. I want to know what's coming, know what to expect, put away money for it, buy insurance for it, and receive an email confirmation.

What keeps me coming back to my secret screwy worldview is that in a very limited way and for small pockets of time, it works, so it tricks me over and over into believing in my own ability to save my own life. I respect people who pray, and who appear to be living that wiggly, whatever-God-wants kind of life, but it's sort of how I respect people who don't believe in conventional medicine—it's indie and cool, but when I'm feeling a little under the weather, I want every machine and tube and drug in the world.

The problem is that the worldview I've chosen has melted like butter. I had a plan, and the plan is gone. I did it right, in my own made-up system, and it all came out wrong. All my logic and contingencies and smoke alarms and insurance didn't see this coming, and now my life has changed. I'm off the plan. And I loved the plan. I believed in the plan, secretly, way more devoutly than I believed in the mysterious work of God.

So now, out of desperation, I'm back to prayer. I'm back to prayer, sheepishly, because I couldn't make my life work without it. I pray out of sheer lack of options.

This is my most basic, most frequent, starting place prayer: *Dear God, I need help. I can't make it anymore. Can you please give me a little something for the pain?*

Last spring, we had five funerals in five weeks, between the church in our hometown and our church in Grand Rapids. None were natural causes, not elderly people at the end of their well-spent lives. A sick six-month-old baby, two suicides, two accidents, 18, 20, 21, 22 years old.

At our housechurch that week, we just stared at each other, exhausted, spent, cried-out, sliced open. One of the women broke the silence by saying, "To be honest, when we pray as a group, I don't pray. If God's going to heal someone because of prayers, there are enough people praying. I don't know if I believe one more voice matters."

I didn't know what to say to her, but what I do know is this: prayer helps me. When I pray, something freaked-out and dazed inside me finds a place to lay down and rest. When I pray, I don't feel so alone in the universe. I feel like there is a web, a finely-spun net, holding it all together, keeping it spinning. I feel powerless, and prayer reminds me that I may be powerless, but there is power, and the one who holds the power is good. Prayer reminds me that the universe is not powerless against the evil and loss that seems to be swallowing up this season in our community.

I imagine a huge choir, hundreds of voices, and they're singing something unquestionably, remarkably beautiful, and if you look at each person, you can see their intensity, their attention to detail and precision, their extreme focus on sounds and phrases. And you can see their love for music and their passion to sing. You could never pick out an individual voice, out of those several hundred, but that's not the point. They are not singing to be heard individually. They are singing for the act itself, for the love of music and tone and melody. That's one of the reasons I pray, for the act itself.

I pray because I need to. Because I need to remind myself that there is something up there and that it is good. I pray to be heard, certainly, but practically speaking, what the act of prayer does in my life is profound in its own right. The act and posture of prayer connects me back to something

I lose so often, something that gets snipped like a string. Prayer ties up the string one more time. Prayer says, I know you're up there. I believe you. I can make it. I know you are good. To pray is to say that there is more than I can see, and more than I can do. There is more going on than meets the eye.

Prayer heals all the muscles that I've been clenching for a long time, while I'm holding it together, gritting my teeth, waiting for impact. Prayer, like yoga, like singing, brings soft from hard, pliant from brittle, possible from impossible, warm from cold, breath from breathless. And no matter what gets you there, it is better to be there than not.

confession

On Monday night at housechurch, a very unfortunate thing happened. Before dinner, right at the beginning of the night, someone mentioned a friend of ours, and mentioned, offhandedly, casually, that this friend of ours is meeting with a publisher about writing a book. And then we talked about other things, normal things. We ate pizza from JB's, our very favorite pizza place. We gobbled up the pizza and caught up on our lives, and I was a part of the conversation in some vague way, nodding and interjecting occasionally. But there was a whole other thing going on inside me while I pretended to smile and listen.

While we talked, I was being absolutely consumed, eaten from the inside out with jealousy, like a million termites were eating out my bones and organs and I was about to turn to dust, hollow and dry. This was not a brief passing stab of jealousy that slices for a moment and then fades back into all the other things you vaguely wish were different in the course of a day. This was jealousy like a house fire, something you absolutely cannot ignore and something that might send you to the emergency room. I could feel my eyes becoming small and beady and my soul shrinking down to a tiny wrinkled peach pit.

I am not unfamiliar with jealousy. But usually I can play the game and feel a little better. You know the game — you think of the thing you have that they don't, to make yourself feel better. You tell yourself that even though he has boatloads of money, at least you have a loving family instead of being a sad, lonely, soulless Scrooge of a person, which makes you feel a little better about driving a '92 Camry. Or you tell yourself that she may have a genuinely perfect body, like a computer generated image, but unfortunately she's got the personality of a dirty Kleenex, unlike your empathetic, kind self.

The terrible thing that happened to me Monday night is that I realized there is a person in my life against whom I cannot win the game. I thought I was holding her off, and Monday night, she beat me. Badly. For starters, she is more attractive than I am, in a way that's not even a judgment call, like the way the ocean is more attractive than a landfill. She is skilled in areas in which I can't even pretend a vague understanding, let alone competence. Math, for example, and parallel parking. She drives the kind of car I drive in the movies in my head. She fits into the jeans I fit into in the movies in my head.

I held it together for a long time, just by a thread, because she really is a dear friend of mine, and because, secretly, I held tightly and grabbily to the fact that although she is a shining, amazing person on every count, she probably will never write a book. Secretly, I thought, I will write a book and will hold that book out like Kryptonite — ha! ha! I wrote a book! You're gorgeous? I wrote a book! People who don't invite me to their parties always invite you? I wrote a book!

It was the last tiny bit of ground I had to stand on, because she had me in every single other area. And then, Monday night, someone happened to mention that she's writing a book, too. It made me want to pray. And by pray, I mean stand up in the middle of dinner and shake my fist at God and demand, "How *could* you?" I fastened my mind on it throughout dinner, spiraling rapidly down and down and down until I almost couldn't speak. On one hand, I was so mad that this person could not leave me alone, could not just leave me the one tiny shred I had left and let me be the one who writes books. Isn't it enough to be glowingly attractive? Can't you just parallel park your cool car and cook your fabulous meals from scratch, and let me be the one who writes a book? And then on the other hand, at the same moment, I was painfully aware that I was in dangerous territory, spiritually. I was very, very ashamed of myself. This is a person I love. And I am so jealous of her that I can't even eat my pizza.

After dinner, Annette and Sarah and I were sitting on the couch, and I blurted out that I had to tell them something. I said, "If that person writes a book, I will have to go to therapy twenty-four hours a day for the rest of my life. I am literally overflowing with jealousy. This person is better than me at every single thing, and I can't make it if she writes a book."

I waited for them to get up and leave, to look at each other and giggle and walk out the door, or stare at me like I'm a murderer and scooch away from me on the couch. They're really good people—mature, godly people who don't have shriveled up souls or beady eyes like I do. They listened, and they didn't leave. We talked about it for a few minutes, and I asked them maybe not to tell their husbands about it, because I felt small and ashamed, and not ready for them to know that part of me yet, or maybe ever. We talked about some other unrelated things, and then I brought it back to my creepy self one more time. "Remember, um, remember that thing I told you, that terrible thing? Do you think you can still love me?" They said, very seriously, that they could, and I scooched a little closer to them on the couch, like I was a small child who felt safe and protected, because I did.

That secret drove me nuts all through dinner, and then when I let it out, when I confessed to my friends, something released in my chest. It felt terrifying and risky to tell them something like that, but at the same time, it felt right, like after I said it, it didn't have as much power as it did before. I still need to do some quite serious work on my insides, some stripping and sanding and refinishing, but when I told my secret, I felt my soul expand, just a tiny bit, like it had been holding its breath for a long time and finally got to breathe again.

I've never practiced confession the way Catholics do, although one of my favorite parts of Catholic weddings is that even though there's a wedding going on, people can still come to confess. A friend of mine got married in a gorgeous Catholic church in Chicago. The flowers and the music were grand, and the guests were just dressed to the nines, and then I noticed a woman at the end of one of the pews, with curlers in her hair and slippers on, clutching her purse close to her, like she was at the bus station, and not at a black-tie wedding ceremony, and like she thought someone might try to swipe it. I whispered to one of my friends, and she whispered back that no matter what's happening in the church, you can always confess, even during a wedding ceremony.

I don't know what that woman came to confess, if she did something really bad and couldn't wait, or if that was her standing appointment and we were cramping her style. But I do know how it feels to really desperately need to confess, like your insides are filling up with black smoke and you just have to let it out, and quick. I know what it feels like to carry something with you that's eating you alive, and I know the weightless, wondrous feeling of letting it out, one tiny baby step back toward the person you want to be.

shalom

There is a way of living, a way of harmonizing and hitting a balance point, a converging of a thousand balance points and voices, layering together, twisting together, and there are moments when it all clicks into place just for a split second—God and marriage and forgiveness and something deep inside that feels like peace—and that's the place I'm trying to get to.

I have glimpses every once in a while of this achingly beautiful way of living that comes when the plates stop spinning and the masks fall off and the apologies come from the deepest places and so do the prayers, and I am fighting, elbowing to make more of my life that life. I want that spirit or force of happiness that is so much deeper than happy—peace that comes from your toes, that makes you want to live forever, that makes you gulp back sobs because you remember so many moments of so much un-peace. I search for those moments the way I search for beach glass, bits of glitter along a desolate expanse of sand, and I want those moments to stretch into hours, into days.

The word I use for it is *shalom*. It is the physical, sense-oriented, relational, communal, personal, ideological posture that arches God-ward. That's the best way I can describe it. It's equilibrium and free-fall, balance and shake. It's a new dance, a new taste, the feeling of falling in love, the knowledge of being set free. It's that split-second cross between a fact and a feeling, something you would swear on in a court of law but couldn't find words for if you tried.

To get there, I'm finding, is the hardest work and the most worthwhile fight. Shalom requires so much, so much more than I thought I would have to sacrifice, and it scrapes so deeply through the lowest parts of me, divulging and demonstrating so many dark corners. It's something you can't fake, so you have to lay yourself open to it, wide open and vulnerable to what it might ask of you, what it might require you to give up, get over, get outside of, get free from. It feels, sometimes, like running farther than you thought you could run, legs shaking and lungs burning, feeling proud and surprised at what little old you can do.

The spirit and the soul and the body and the mind are all connected, even though we've chosen to segment them, thinking things would stay more organized that way, like a cafeteria tray with compartments for pudding and green beans. But when we're chopped apart, we lose the essence, the possibility of being aligned, connected, multiplying out into something more than legs and math formulas we learned in high school.

Shalom is about God, and about the voice and spirit of God blowing through and permeating all the dark corners that we've chopped off, locked down. It's about believing, and letting belief move you to forgive. It's about grace, and letting grace propel you into action. It's about the whole of our lives becoming woven through with the sacred spirit of God, through friendship and confession, through rest and motion, through marriage and silence.

Shalom is the act of life lifting up and becoming an act of worship and celebration, a sacrament, an offering. It's about living in a world of movie theaters and shoes and highways and websites, and finding those things to be shot through with the same spirit and divinity and possibility that we see in ourselves. It's living with purpose and sacrifice and intention, willing to be held to the highest, narrowest possible standard of goodness, and in the same breath, finding goodness where most people see nothing but dirt.

I have been surprised to find that I am given more life, more hope, more moments of buoyancy and redemption, the more I give up. The more I let go, do without, reduce, the more I feel rich. The more I let people be who they are, instead of cramming them into what I need from them, the more surprised I am by their beauty and depth.

When we can manage to live this way of shalom, even for a moment, we pull each other up toward something bigger, wider, more beautiful, because left to my own devices, chances are, I will spiral down until life is nothing more than the mildew smell on my kitchen towels and the guilt I feel about all the things I thought I'd be.

The truest thing, it seems, is the biggest: the big idea of making a life with God, with honor, with honesty and community and beauty and the fragile delicate recipe of those, searching for the place where they all come together, where hope and struggle and beauty and tears swirl together into the best, brightest moments of life. That's what I believe about God.

I believe life is a bottle rocket, a celebration, and it requires everything we have, and it demands that we battle through fear and resentment, and it demands that we release our need to be the best, the prettiest, the most perfect and together, because the big thing, the forceful beautiful thing is happening already, all around us, and we might miss it if we're too busy meeting our parents' expectations or winning awards.

Shalom is happening all around us, but it never happens on its own. The best things never do happen on their own, and shalom is the very best thing. In the same way that forgiveness never feels natural until after it's done, and hope always feels impossible before we commit to it, in the same way that taking is easier than giving, and giving in is easier than getting up, in that same way, shalom never happens on its own.

It happens when we do the hardest work, the most secret struggle, the most demanding truth telling. In those moments of ferocity and fight, peace is born. Shalom arrives, and everything is new. And when you've tasted it, smelled it, fought for it, labored it into life, you'll give your soul to get a little more, and it is always worth it.

Shalom.

good causes

Today my friend, Julie, who takes good care of me, who takes good care of everyone, let me bring her dinner. Her husband, Doug, had two very scary seizures in the last two days, and a zillion tests and scans and appointments with neurologists. They had just come home from the hospital, and they were sitting on the front porch when I drove up, and Lilly, their three-year-old, was riding her big-girl bike on the sidewalk in her pink underpants.

It was ninety-four degrees today, and they were exhausted. We sat on the porch and ate salads with big chunks of tomato and cilantro and black beans, and drank cold chardonnay, the wine glasses sweating in the heat. Lilly entertained us, and we told stories and sat in silence for long moments. As I drove away, after Julie kissed me on the cheek in the doorway, I realized that may have been my favorite moment with their family.

There is something about summer in Michigan that feels heady and reckless and celebratory, and then something about the pain and fear of hospitals and emergency phone calls that brings everything to Technicolor, and lets a whole lot of things fall away, leaving you with the barest bones, the things that matter when nothing else does, like your three-year-old in her underwear, and your husband, healthy.

The last three months have been about death and fights and weddings and babies and tears, and it feels like the plain old moments of life that normally buffer these huge, sweeping events got edited out, and all these big life things got squished together, one after another after another. Before I went over to Julie's today, I unpacked my bags. There were four of them, from four different trips in the last three weeks. I felt like an archaeologist, unearthing layer after layer of the chronology of the month. I did an insane amount of laundry, as though a football team lived here, instead of just Aaron and me, and I went grocery shopping for the first time in weeks.

Being with Julie and Doug today made me think about the idea that everything is okay. That idea is nothing but cruel in its untruth. Okayness is a thin scab that rips off every once in a while and exposes a river of blood and infection, an inroad to the whole body. We live in reasonable peace, accomplishing things and doing what we're told and expecting that if we behave, we will be rewarded; that for living quietly and industriously, for donating to Easter Seals and letting people merge in front of us on the highway, we will be given good things, good lives. And then something happens to us; we get that phone call or that feeling or that doctor's report, and everything changes.

The sky might as well be red, the solid ground replaced with seawater, because it is a different world. It's like a chemical change, charges reversing from positive to negative. And in the midst of this change, you look around and realize that everyone else seems to be doing fine, that you must be the only one who notices this change.

We preserve the myth even though we no longer believe it. We insist that everything is okay. But we're kidding ourselves. Can you look into the eyes of the people around you and really believe that everything is okay? We want to believe that things roll off our backs, that we are tough and world-wise, and that we're all holding it together pretty well. But you know which door you lock behind you when you're crying so hard you can't see. You know what word or image rips off that scab. Everything is not okay.

In all of my scrambling to do the right thing and be the right person, I miss some of the most important things I think God might be asking me to do. For a lot of different reasons, for the better part of the last several years, I have been way too busy for interruptions. I worked and worked on behalf of a good cause, at the expense of all the things I would have seen if I had slowed down enough to look around my life. I wanted to be productive and useful and focused, and I turned into someone who was frazzled and scattered, and who could not bear the emotional weight of her own life, let alone someone else's. I don't want to be that person. And I'm ashamed that I let myself move so far from who I wanted to be.

This week, listening to God and doing what it seemed like he was asking looked a lot like doing nothing, really. I changed plans and bought gifts and said prayers and made a little bed on the couch for my friend who needed a soft place for the night, and the most important thing about this is that there is nothing particularly noble or difficult about anything I did. I did the average things that needed to be done in the lives of the people around me. And I'm in a really good mood about the whole thing, because I think I'm catching on to something that God wanted from me all along.

The bottom just falls out sometimes, and nobody is exempt. Everything is not okay. And one of the most sacred gifts we can offer before God is the willingness to make a bed on the couch or make a phone call or make a meal or make a sacrifice for someone we care about. What else is there to do? I can't take away the seizures, although I would if I could. I can't tell Lilly that it's never going to happen again, although I would if I could. But I can be there, and I can feed them, and I can listen to their stories, of funny things the doctors said, and the strange and infuriating things that family members invariably say in tense situations. I can sit in silence in the heat and stillness of a sticky June night, knowing that everything is not okay, but that this tiny moment is.

I'm giving it a shot, because this week it feels like the most spiritually right thing I've done for a while, and I feel a little bit prouder of myself, a little bit closer to the person that I want to be, a little bit like a kid being given a little job to do and doing it well. This might be the big, important work, the good cause I've been looking for.

Out of the thousands of parties and picnics and dinners I've spent with Doug and Julie and Lilly, there was a quality to the time I spent with them tonight; maybe because of the exhaustion and the urgency and the heat. It is placed firmly in my memory like an old picture, and as I think of it, I feel thankful, and when I wonder about what matters, in our lives and our friendships and our families and in the good causes we believe in, I know this night did.

the hook

When I'm trying to forgive someone, I picture myself physically lifting that person off a big hook, like in a cartoon. I never want to. I prefer to stew and focus my anger on them like a laser pointer, and wish them illnesses and bad skin. I hope that they will get fat and people will talk behind their backs and their toilets will overflow and their computers will crash. I work on my anger toward them like I'm working on a loose tooth with my tongue, back and forth. I work on it like I'm training for the Olympics, with tremendous dedication and force.

Earlier this year, a friend of mine made me really mad. Crazy mad. My (genius) therapist suggests that crazy mad is always covering over hurt and fear, so if we're telling the whole truth here, she hurt me, and she made me feel scared. And that's worse than just making me mad. I felt small and scared and out of control, and I felt like my friend was making decision after decision to hurt me. Every time I heard from her or about her, it hurt. It was like there was sharp glass on her hands, and every time she got near me, she cut me, even if she swore she didn't mean to.

For a while, it brought me so much joy to be angry with her and to put her back up on the hook, over and over.

It's like I was a giant, hovering over tiny little regular people, laughing with glee as I put her on the hook again and again. I felt powerful, I think, like I could control her and hurt her the way she hurt me. I exhausted myself imagining the same conversation again and again, but slightly different each time, saying clever things and finding loopholes in her lame arguments. I was the captain of the debate team in my mind, and I was extremely busy debating her.

Sarah asked me how I was doing one night when I went over to her house to take a walk with her. "Well," I said, "it's been pretty hard lately with my friend at whom I am very angry." I don't call her that. I call her by her name, but I'm not going to tell you her name. There was a time when I would have given you her name, cell phone number, and directions to her house so you could have a little word with her on my behalf, along with an itemized list of her faults in descending order of severity, but now I just call her "my friend at whom I am very angry."

So I told Sarah that we had been having a hard time lately. "Oh," she said. "When did you talk to her?" I rolled my eyes and puffed out my breath like I was a seventh grade girl. I didn't *talk* to her. Was she crazy? "I, um, I actually didn't talk with her at all. I mean, it's been hard … in my head."

Gently, kindly, she paused, waiting for me to realize what I just said. "Hard in your head?" Again, gently, kindly. I had been spending hours in imaginary conversations, tying myself up in knots, harboring secret fantasies of this person at whom I am very angry falling down in public, planning out elaborate comebacks I should have actually said months ago.

I kept thinking about her, and the anger and the venom were starting to feel familiar. First I thought about what happened. And then the muscles in my neck and back scrunched up, and I felt bad at the base of my skull. Even if lots of other parts of life were going well, there was this thing, this tightness in my shoulders and my neck. Then it got harder to breathe, and it felt like something was rotting inside me, the way something goes bad in the refrigerator.

The thing that keeps me going with the anger and the rotten feelings is that I think I'm right. Really. When I think about what happened, I think she did a bad thing to a not entirely bad person named me. And I want her to have to apologize. Loudly. Publicly. And give me a present, too. I want her to feel how bad I felt, how small and scared. I want her to tell me she was wrong, and promise never to do anything like that again, in writing, with a notary public present.

And I think if we went to court, some strange friendship court where you can get a ruling about these things, I think I would win, still, even after all these months. The pain has softened ever so slightly, but it still seems like she did something wrong. How do I forgive someone who doesn't think she did anything wrong? Or who doesn't care?

I could maybe do it if she groveled or begged. It would be even easier if she cried a lot. I would be more apt to forgive her if she told me she thought I was a genius with great fashion sense and that she wants to be like me someday. But nothing. No phone calls. No emails. No large, fragrant bouquets of flowers. Nothing. Why would I forgive someone who doesn't even think she needs to be forgiven?

This is why. Because I want my neck and my back muscles to stop hurting, to unfurl like window shades. Because I want to sleep instead of having endless imaginary conversations. Because I want my mind back. Because I want my life back. Because she's not the only one on the hook. Because every time I hang her up on that hook, the hook reaches down and grabs me, too.

When I told Sarah that things had been hard in my head, I realized that I'm the only one suffering right now. My anger doesn't hurt the person at whom I am very angry, but it hurts me. My friend Rory says something like bitterness is when you drink poison hoping the other person dies. My friend is doing great, I think, but I stagger around in a fog of anger and clenched jaws and fists, waiting for a showdown that will never come and an apology that will never be offered.

So I let her off the hook. I let her off once, to start, and felt pretty good about myself, until someone brought up her name at lunch, and then I got mad all over again, which threw me for a loop. I *forgave* her. Why am I still so mad at her? I felt like I bought expensive wrinkle cream and woke up more wrinkly than ever. I wanted my money back.

I realized that I had to take her off the hook every single time, not just one big time. I had to take her off the hook in the morning, and then again at lunch, when someone gave me a new reason to be mad at her. Over and over, all day, I had to do the heavy lifting work of letting her off the hook. It was like moving a piano all the way across the living room, and then waking up the next morning and finding that it's back in the other corner, and I have to move it again. Every day I had to push that heavy piano all the way across the living room, even though I just did it the day before. It was like a full-time job, forgiving her over and over, with each new angry thought or bad conversation, but it was good work, like how good it feels to shovel snow or rake leaves in the cold air.

And I still have to keep letting her off, every day, sometimes several times a day. Not for her sake, but for mine, because I want off the hook. It's hard work, and I don't want to do it, but I keep doing it. I keep letting her off the hook, because when I do, I can breathe again.

how sweet it is

My parents' first date was a walk on the pier in South Haven, Michigan, a tiny town on the lakeshore. Both grew up spending summer nights and weekends there, both their fathers were sailors. It was on that same stretch of lakeshore that I learned to swim, learned to windsurf, learned to sail, learned to dive. It was in that same town that I got my first job, left my first tooth under my pillow for the tooth fairy. Now it is the town where we will teach our children to take their first steps, where they will play in the sand for the first time, where they will swing for the first time on the swings at North Beach.

The end of the summer always turns us to nostalgia, and inevitably by Labor Day weekend, we start our list of the best moments of the summer. One year we declared the best moment was when, after three cold and rainy days of Memorial Day weekend, with each boat full of shivering, wet, disappointed guests, we abandoned ship and opened the yacht club, the only dry place left, and climbed behind the bar to mix drinks, leaving a tab for the staff to bill us later. We spread our wet jackets and fleeces over the chandeliers to dry, and left soggy footprints all over the tile behind the bar.

Another summer, the best moment was when our friend Troy brought new meaning to the term "belly flop." Responding to a challenge on a cloudless, hot Sunday afternoon, he flopped so hard and so comprehensively that every part of his body, from the top of his bald head to the tops of his feet, was gleaming red. We still talk about Troy and his famous belly flop. Honorable mention that year, I believe, goes to the string of important items dropped overboard in the course of a weekend—one pair of sunglasses, two cell phones, an iPod, and a ring. We're pretty sure that if we ever dredged the river near our slip, we'd find a decade of my sunglasses and my brother's cell phones, as well as lots of people's car keys.

This summer, the moment was easy to pick and unanimous. On a clear Saturday night in July, in the backyard of their house with the very best view in town, looking over the river and out onto the lake, our dear friends Jim and Jodi were married. The bride was preceded down the aisle by her son and daughters and grandchildren, and the groom surrounded by his sailing buddies, among them my brother. She was stunning in pale gold satin, and he looked every bit the dashing sailor in linen shorts. The backyard was a glorious riot of candles and flowers and tan shoulders and summer dresses, and one friend made sushi and another baked brie and another served champagne. Aaron played the guitar and sang "How Sweet It Is" as they walked down the aisle in the fading light. It was a true family operation: my dad performed the ceremony, and my mom and I helped with the food and served drinks under a wide umbrella, lit from underneath with twinkling lights. It was an evening of happy tears and great celebration for two people, but more than that, for one new family that has been born and grown and nurtured over the last five years, right in this backyard, and on the river, and on the beach.

In the vows they wrote for one another, Jim talked about his life before Jodi, and how deeply he valued his independence. When he said it, we all laughed, because it was the understatement of the decade, like saying Janis Joplin valued a good cocktail. Watching Jim become a partner and companion, and more than that, a father and grandfather, has been a moving and very surprising transformation, and he's more surprised than anyone. For years, he's worked and traveled and built a company and skied and sailed on his own schedule, at his own whim.

And then came Jodi, this gorgeous woman whose deepest commitment is to her children and grandchildren, and the life she invited him into was more about Santa than ski season and more about naptime than staying out all night. And although there have been some parts of himself that he has left behind, those of us who love him know that the man who stood before Jodi that night is the best Jim we've ever known, and that what he gave up is nothing in comparison to what he has gained.

Last summer, Kaj, Jodi's grandson, was on the boat with Todd and my dad and me, and I asked him conspiratorially, "Kaj, you can tell me the truth: who do you think is better at driving the boat, Todd or Bill?" And he looked at one and then the other, and he said, "Jim!" Jim's name wasn't even in the running that day, but for Kaj, it always is.

That night, Jim became a father and a grandfather, although really, Jim became Kaj's papa long before the wedding. He became his papa little by little over five summers, playing in the sand and jumping off the boat and making sure Kaj's life jacket was buckled right every time.

Just after the ceremony, back in the house for a moment, Jodi's daughter, Josilyn, hugged Jim. "Hi, Dad," she said, trying to make it sound casual. Neither of them was fooled.

"I've been waiting to say that for such a long time!" she said through her tears. Just about as long as he'd been waiting to hear it.

In the same way that he became Kaj's papa little by little over five years, he'd become Josilyn's dad that way, too, on snowboarding trips and boat rides, helping with homework and watching her games.

That night didn't feel like a beginning, the way that some weddings do. It felt better than that. It felt like a celebration for something that began a long time ago, and like what we were doing that night was stopping to notice and celebrate this glorious thing that had been inching its way into existence day by day, growing like a slender tough stalk, almost imperceptibly, until one day you realize it's become a strong tall tree, providing shade and protection to everyone under its branches.

There's something about a marriage of adults, people who own homes and businesses and have families and patterns and traditions. Of course, there is something so sweet and shining about a young bride and groom, and their first home and first dishes and first set of towels. But there is a different beauty and a different force when two people who have been down that road far enough to hit some bumps decide to bend themselves once again toward partnership. Where there was naïveté, here there is sobriety. Where a young bride leaves her family, an older bride brings hers with her. Where a young groom hopes all goes well, an older groom knows what to do when it doesn't.

That night felt sacred and beautiful and imbued with
something heavy. It was a hard-won celebration, a willingness
to re-believe in love, to fall again, to teach and be taught, to
enter through a door both had believed was closed forever.
We danced and ate cake and toasted them with champagne
and told crazy old sailing stories, for our own benefit,
certainly, since every person there had heard them all a
million times. We laughed and let the kids stay up way too
late and watched the bobbing mast lights on the sailboats in
the harbor, hypnotized by them and by the beauty and hope
of that night.

blessings and curses

There are things that happen to us, and when they happen, they give us two options. Either way, we will never be the same, and we shouldn't. These things can either strip us down to the bone and allow us to become strong and honest, or they can be the reasons we use to behave poorly indefinitely, the justification for all manner of broken relationships and broken ideals. It could be the thing that allows everything else to turn, that allows the lock of our lives to finally spring open and our pent-up selves to blossom like preening flowers. Or it can be the reason we use to justify our anger and the sharp tones in our voices for the rest of our lives.

One of my dearest and oldest friends, Jon, married a girl I grew up with. In the middle of the night two years later, Jon called me because he had just found emails that made it clear to him that his wife was cheating on him. Soon after, she left and never came back. Less than a year later, they were divorced, and the day they went to court, we threw a party for Jon, not to celebrate the fact of the divorce, but because it didn't seem right that he would go home to their empty apartment after the courthouse. We grilled out and drank icy margaritas with salty rims, and sat on the back steps of our townhouse, watching the bugs circle the porch light.

Jon had every right, you could say, to let his life be defined by that day, by that year, by that woman, by that betrayal. But what he did instead was a marvelous thing to watch. He laid himself open and vulnerable to life and God and therapy and close friends, and began the breathtaking process of becoming more than what he had been in a thousand different ways. He is softer, in the best possible way, and when you talk to him, you know that he's been down to the bottom and fought his way back up. He listens more closely and prays like he's talking to a best friend. I knew him well for years before she left, and although I would never wish upon anyone the searing pain I saw written on his face during that season, what God did in his life through that event makes me believe in God's goodness even more than I did before.

In May, three years ago, I stood at the back of a church and cried great big happy tears as he married Christina, a beautiful and smart woman who loves him with a steadiness that feels like a sailboat's keel. There's something immovable in her, and it feels like just the right thing for the zig-zag path of his life. Their sons, Gabe and Will, are darling gray-eyed miracles, and when I see Jon with them, I know that it seemed like God was being cruel that year, that middle of the night when he called me. But he was not. What I know now is that his kindness burns through even the deepest betrayals and invites life from death every chance we let him. There are things that explode into our lives and we call them curses, and then one day, a year later or ten years later, we realize that they are actually something else. They are the very most precious kinds of blessings.

It's dark today, almost like night and cool and rainy. It always seems in the dead of summer that it will be summer forever, that it couldn't possibly ever get cold again. And then there are days like today that remind you that it will. The leaves are starting to change, and the clouds have a decidedly different presence than the one they had all summer. They are brighter, more aggressive, fighting the sun more directly than the summer clouds who seemed more content to let the sun lead the way. These clouds mean business.

The slight turn of seasons reminds me of last fall, and it strikes me that my life has changed almost beyond recognition since then. In the process of breaking my heart, life or God or something—not that I don't believe God moves in these ways, I just don't want to immediately blame him for a crime he didn't commit—also delivered me to the life I've been wanting. And I can spend all my life and all my soul and all my words on the pain of what happened to me, or I can take this glimmering gift and run.

The day I left my job at the church was the darkest day of my life so far. It felt like a curse, a punch in the face, a slice to the core. It made me feel like my luck had run out cosmically, and from then on, all I could expect was rain.

But the only person who decided my life had turned to dust was me. The only person who is still deeply troubled about what I've lost, even in the face of what I've gained, is me. I would never have wanted it this way, but something bright and beautiful has been given to me, and I'm in grave danger of losing it, squandering it, becoming a person who cannot find the goodness that's right in front of her because of the sadness that she chooses to let obscure it.

Now we're talking about celebration. Celebration when you think you're calling the shots? Easy. Celebration when your plan is working? Anyone can do that. But when you realize that the story of your life could be told a thousand different ways, that you could tell it over and over as a tragedy, but you choose to call it an epic, that's when you start to learn what celebration is. When what you see in front of you is so far outside of what you dreamed, but you have the belief, the boldness, the courage to call it beautiful instead of calling it wrong, that's celebration.

When you can invest yourself deeply and unremittingly in the life that surrounds you instead of declaring yourself out of the game once and for all, because what's happened to you is too bad, too deep, too ugly for anyone to expect you to move on from, that's that good, rich place. That's the place where the things that looked for all intents and purposes like curses start to stand up and shimmer and dance, and you realize with a gasp that they may have been blessings all along. Or maybe not. Maybe they were curses, in fact, but the force of your belief and your hope and your desperate love for life as it is actually unfolding, has brought a blessing from a curse, like water from a stone, like life from a tomb, like the actual story of God over and over.

I would never try to tell you that every bad thing is really a good thing, just waiting to be gazed at with pretty new eyes, just waiting to be shined up and—ta da!—discovered as fantastic. But what I know is that for me, and for my friend Jon, and for a lot of the people I love, we're discovering that lots of times, not every time, maybe, but more often than not, there is something just past the heartbreak, just past the curse, just past the despair, and that thing is beautiful. You don't want it to be beautiful, at first. You want to stay in the pain and the blackness because it feels familiar, and because you're not done feeling victimized and smashed up. But one day you'll wake up surprised and humbled, staring at something you thought for sure was a curse and has revealed itself to be a blessing—a beautiful, delicate blessing.

There have been a thousand moments when I have felt the weight and the sadness of this season, appropriately. But then there have been some moments where I have felt the blessing and beauty of it, too. Seeing our baby's face on the ultrasound, eating ice cream with Aaron, having breakfast at Annette's and taking Spence for a walk, walking on the pier by myself today after lunch at the Phoenix Street Café. There is a particular beauty to this season, not the obvious everything-is-perfect beauty, but a strange slanted pleasantness that surprises me and catches in my throat like a sob or a song.

Nothing good comes easily. You have to lose things you thought you loved, give up things you thought you needed. You have to get over yourself, beyond your past, out from under the weight of your future. The good stuff never comes when things are easy. It comes when things are all heavily weighted down like moving trucks. It comes just when you think it never will, like a shimmering Las Vegas rising up out of the dry desert, sparkling and humming with energy, a blessing that rose up out of a bone-dry, dusty curse.

When I lived in Santa Barbara, every time I drove to Las Vegas, I always got scared that I was lost, that I would die in the desert, eaten by a coyote. The road was desolate and the truck stops eerie and silent, and I always began to lose hope—there was no Vegas, no city in this bleak desert. We were sure to die, right on the side of the Pearblossom Freeway. And then, every time, there it was, like a mirage, like a happy ending.

We become who we are in these moments. I have a friend who falls back, whenever things are too hard, to an event in her life that happened over a decade ago. It's the thing that she uses to justify cruel behavior, wrecked relationships, terrifying swings of emotion. But wouldn't it be great, wouldn't it be just like God, if that terrible thing could be the thing that lifts her up and delivers her to her best, truest self? I know it can, because it happens all the time, because it happened to my friend Jon, and because it happened to me.

IV

mother prayers

After Henry was born, the first night that we were
home from the hospital, Aaron and I laid in bed just listening
to him breathe. We had a tiny crib that fit flush against our
bed, so that I could feed him in the night. I wanted to be able
to see him a little bit, so I told Aaron I wanted to sleep with
my reading lamp on, just for the first night. I laid down in
the glare of the lamp, peering into the little crib at him, but
I didn't have my contacts in, so I couldn't really see a thing.
What's the point of having the lights on if you can't tell if it's a
baby or a loaf of bread? So I put my glasses on and felt a lot
better about the situation.

Two of my dearest friends, Ruth and Sara, came over
to see him the next day, bearing sleepers and onesies and
board books. They fought over him and snuggled with him
the way mothers do, staring down at him, remembering
when their own sons, now big and squirmy tough boys, were
so tiny. They asked me if I slept all right the night before.
I told them, you know, I didn't sleep great. They looked
concerned, but like they understood, since it was just the first
night. Maybe, I said, um, maybe it was because I slept with
the light on and my glasses on. They laughed hard, and gave

me strict instructions for the next night. At some point in the night, they said, I had to turn the light totally out, and we could work on having it out longer and longer until it was out all night.

Henry was born in October, but it was unseasonably cold, and it snowed the week he came home. In our drafty old house, I was just a touch worried about keeping him warm. Our baby monitor has a temperature display, and I carried it around the house, checking for cold spots, and woke up in the night in a panic every hour or so, afraid that the boiler had stopped, and the space heater had stopped, and that our little boy was turning into a little icicle. To ensure that this wasn't the case, I set the heat in our room high enough to bake a cake, and between the raging space heater and the raging hormones, I roasted all night, like we were in a tribal sweat lodge. Aaron was furious and confused and hot and tired, but knew better than to cross a woman so cranky and fearful, with enough hormones to fuel a rocketship. They should give postpartum hormones to foot soldiers and astronauts and professional football players who need to pump up their game. Aaron was delighted and relieved when the pediatrician finally told us that if we were comfortable, chances are the baby would be comfortable. I inched the heat down further and further until it became reasonable for all three of us, which ended up being about fifteen degrees from where we started.

One snowy Monday, when he was almost three months old, after a busy week and weekend, Henry and I stayed home and wore our pajamas all day. I did laundry while he napped, and while he was awake, we played together. He has a new thing that just kills me. When I stick my tongue out, he sticks his tongue out, and then smiles and laughs, a gurgly drooling laugh, where his blue eyes flash and I'm convinced that he knows a lot more than he lets on. There are moments when I swear he understands every word I say, because he looks up at me with a face that seems to say, "I hear you. I get what you're saying, Mom." We stuck out our tongues for hours. He'll probably grow up to be the next Gene Simmons.

When I change him, I talk with him about the day, about current events, about celebrity breakups. That day, we were discussing Gwen and Gavin's baby, Kingston, and how he looks so remarkably like Gavin. Before I put his sleeper back on, I tickled his legs and belly, and I bent down and kissed the bottoms of his feet, because they're so soft and perfect and chubby, and before I knew it, there were tears running down my face, and I cried so hard, I couldn't keep talking to him.

All alone in our house with my son, in the midst of a frantic holiday season, I knew that that moment right there, in the dim corner of the living room on a dark Monday afternoon, that was the merriest Christmas moment for me. The sweetest moment of gratitude and hope happened right then, in our quiet house with my son, kissing his little baby feet.

And it is, after all, a season for babies. It makes sense to me in a new way that God chose to wrap his divinity in baby bones and baby skin. I always thought maybe it was to demonstrate vulnerability, or to identify fully with each phase of humanity, but now I think it was something else. I think it was because babies make us believe in the possibility and power of the future.

It's genius that the Christ, the Messiah, came as a baby, not because of his helplessness, but because of the possibility every baby holds. We have a regular baby, a non-Christ, non-Messiah baby, and when I look at his sleeping face, all the world seems new and possible.

The world has turned a color I never imagined, and I never dreamed that this little person could capture me so deeply, could change my entire life so completely. This year I lost some things that were very important to me, but in that moment, as I held his little feet, I knew that I had everything the world could possibly give me, that I was richer than a Rockefeller and luckier than a leprechaun. Life sneaks up on us every once in a while and gives us something we didn't even know we wanted, and lights within us a love we didn't even know existed.

I am stunned by the intimacy of this, by the ferocity of feeling. I feel like I could turn inside out if something happened to him, like my mind could melt or my heart stop if he experienced one moment of pain. I want to touch him, hold him, protect him with a panicky, fierce love, like a bear or a dog. I have visceral, wordless feelings that wake me up in the night and make me tremble, and other moments when the world seems so deeply right, so good and perfect, I can't help but pray.

I think babies really do make you believe in God. They make you believe in God because there's something just beyond understanding about their freshness and fragility and their smell and their toes. When they take their first breaths, and when they land, floppy and slippery, on your chest under the bright overhead light in an otherwise dim delivery room, when you watch their tiny sleeping selves, when you hear their thin wild animal cries, you know, you just know in your guts that God is real, and that babies have been with him more recently, have come more directly from him than our worn-out old selves have.

I also believe in God because I have to, because I need someone to pray to with my rabid, sweeping mix of fear and love. I have to believe in something else, I think, or I'd lose my mind. I think I would blow a fuse in my brain every night if I couldn't entrust Henry to God for safekeeping while I sleep. It's hard enough for me to sleep, and I believe very desperately in God. I'd never sleep a wink if I didn't.

Those first nights, I prayed out loud every night, asking God to keep Henry alive through the night. I had no reason to believe that something would happen to him. He was healthy and normal, although at the beginning, healthy and normal seem relative, because they are so tiny and wiggly and alien. So I prayed out loud, fervently, like I was at a revival. Dear God, *please please please* keep our baby healthy and alive through the night. *Thank you thank you thank you* for him, and *please please please* keep him safe through the night. I wasn't creative in my language, but what I lacked in vocabulary, I made up for in intensity. I became downright televangelist in my prayers. Babies must bring out the inner charismatic in all of us.

One of the things you always hear people say about having a child is that you would give your life for them, in a heartbeat, any chance you get. And looking at my son now, that is absolutely, totally true. I'd give up anything at all, and give my life without a moment's thought, if it would keep him safe or healthy.

I'm realizing that there's a horrible problem, though: most likely, I won't get the chance. If I could sign on the back of my license, like how you sign to become an organ donor, I would, right away, and then anytime he was about to get hurt, I could flash my card, and the dog would bite me instead of him. I could flash my card, and the cancer would come to my body and not his. That's how it should be, because I would do it every time. Every parent would. The terrible thing about parenting is that I can't do that. He's going to get sick and going to get hurt, and there's nothing

I can do about it, short of keeping him in a bubble, which I'm still considering.

I remember hearing my mother say that she really learned to pray when I was born, out of necessity and fear. And now I get it. This is my new prayer, my mother-prayer: Dear God, *please please please*, and *thank you thank you thank you*.

the track star

My dad went to kindergarten with Joel Jager, in Kalamazoo, Michigan. They grew up in the same small town, the same church, the same school. When my dad moved to Chicago, he moved with Joel, and they were roommates for years. In the photographs of my first birthday, Joel and my dad's other friends were playing with all my toys, mugging for the camera, scruffy, bearded men in their young twenties, all of them single but my parents, and certainly childless. I was their first little person, first niece or approximation thereof.

In the earliest days of the church they started, when it was a fledgling youth group renting a theater on Sunday mornings, Joel was the first tech director—the only tech director for years and years. He loaded and unloaded the truck thousands of times, getting up while it was still dark on Sunday mornings, waiting till the last person left on Sunday afternoons to tear down the equipment. He's been an audio engineer now at the church for over thirty years, and when I worked there, sometimes we sat together in the booth when he was mixing and I was producing, and it felt like sitting with an uncle, someone who knows your history better than you do, someone who was there for the stories you just hear after the fact, like folklore.

This year, Joel's son, Evan, is a senior in high school. He's a runner, which is putting it mildly. He's a star. He has won every conference meet, every regional meet, and every sectional meet he's run. He won state four times, set several course records, and is fourth in the nation in both the one-mile and two-mile this year. The *Chicago Sun-Times* called Evan quite possibly the best athlete Jacobs High School has ever produced. My husband is a little hurt by this, as a Jacobs alum, and, in his memory, an unsung hero of his sophomore basketball team, but when he heard that Evan ran a 4:05 mile, he grudgingly conceded the title. Evan is a phenomenon, that rare combination of natural talent and determination and discipline and sportsmanship, and because of those things, has become one of the most chronicled and celebrated high school athletes in the country.

This is the thing: his father, Joel, has never run a day in his life. Joel had polio as a small child and walks with a pronounced limp. I remember when I was little, feeling very sad and angry about Uncle Joel's legs, because I wanted him to be healthy and strong, because I wanted him to be happy, because he was so good to me and made me happy.

And now, Evan. What must it be like for Joel to watch his son run? What must it be like for him to look at his son's strong fast legs? How proud and moving it must be for a father to watch a son live a life that was so wholly unavailable to him. I don't pretend to know what it's like to be Joel. I don't know what things are the most difficult to do without, whether it's running or downhill skiing or ballroom dancing. Okay, I know Joel well enough to know that it's not ballroom dancing. I bet a few of the most painful moments might have been when he wanted to play with his kids, to run around with them in the backyard playing tag and hide-and-seek. I know that when he overexerts himself, he pays for it with a lot of pain for several days afterward, and I bet he did that over and over again to play with his kids, and I bet that sometimes the pain was worth it. I don't know. But I do know that Joel is proud of that kid. And that he loves to watch Evan run.

Life feels so tedious sometimes, so lacking in poetry and beauty and connection. We're just ticking away time, waiting for spring, waiting for a sale, waiting for vacation. I was driving, absentmindedly, feeling bland and ground down, near my hometown one day when we were back for a visit. And on the side of Randall Road, almost swallowed up by the glare of parking lot lights for an eternal stretch of Meijer and Petco and Costco and OfficeMax, was a sign. The sign read, *Algonquin, Home of Evan Jager, State Track Champion, 2006, 2007.*

And life clicked back into color, and tears sprang into my eyes. Evan Jager is a track star. How's that for beauty and intervention and sacred hands working behind the scenes, weaving poetry into our lives? It makes me believe in God anew today. That my friend Joel, my dear uncle-friend Joel, has a son who can run. Thank God.

Thank you, God, for the things you heal, the things you redeem, the things you refuse to leave just as they have been for what seems like forever. Thank you for Evan, and for giving to Joel a son who runs. The poetry of that stuns me, and reminds me once again that just when I think we're ticking off days like a to-do list, we're not. We're living the bright, beautiful stuff of movies and love songs, in our backyards and at high school track meets and right on Randall Road.

ladybugs

Having a baby is really hard. I know everyone tells you that. Everyone is right. They should pass out newborns to suspected terrorists, because I guarantee they'd break and give up their secrets in three days flat, after the baby wakes them up every two hours around the clock.

My brother-in-law is the lead singer of a metal band called Eleventh Day. They call themselves Eleventh Day, because, apparently, if you go without sleep for ten full days, on the eleventh day, if you commit a crime, you can plead criminal insanity. If that's true, new parents should be able to commit armed robbery, shrug their shoulders, and point to the carseat in the back of the getaway car. Like we have the energy to commit crimes. I don't even have the energy to tweeze my eyebrows. I look like Woody Allen in a nursing bra these days.

This morning, when I was up with Henry at three, at five, and at seven, I found myself thinking things that seemed to me to be profound, and seemed to flow out of some depth of wisdom given to me now that I am a mother. I wrote them down because lots of writers talk about the importance of capturing thoughts right when they occur, invariably when you're not at your computer. So I have a pad of bright green Post-Its on the nightstand, and after Henry goes back to sleep in the night, I write down these visions that I've been working on while feeding him. The problem is that in the morning, it becomes clear to me that I've lost my mind. The Post-Its say things like, "Iron Chef/poopypants, transition to Exodus." And "How Che Guevara is like Snoopy, tie in cake."

My life is so much quieter now. When you work on a team and you have a boss and projects and deadlines, when you get to the end of something, someone says, "Good job." Or, "Thank you." Or, "Wow, that was smart and helpful." But Henry never looks up at me when I'm changing his diaper and says, "Good move with the wipes, Mom. Very thorough." He doesn't look up at me when I'm trying to get him to go back to sleep in the night and whisper, "Fabulous technique with the shushing and rocking. You're a genius."

It doesn't matter to Henry one little bit that I can speak French or explicate sentences or cook really good roasted salmon. What matters is that I can be there with him as long as he needs me. What matters to him is that I can play with Froggie, his favorite toy, one more time, one more time, one more time.

All my life I've been multitasking. I'm good at it. I don't want to be braggy, but I'm kind of a champion multitasker, really. And all of a sudden, what's valuable is not the multitasking, but the single task—being with him, only him, doing nothing else.

Writing is the same way. I was good at working, good at the buzz and busyness of leading people and managing events and ideas. What made me good at it was my ability to hold so many things in my head, like a handful of ladybugs. And now my work, writing, is about letting all the bugs crawl away and being able to focus on a totally blank page, a totally empty hand. Writing is about choosing the one narrow thing and following it as far as it will take me, instead of chasing all the snaps and crackles in my head.

I thought that each of those single tasks, caring for our baby and writing, would make my world very small. What I have found, though, is that they make my world impossibly big, that they open up something in my head and in my heart.

In my grandparents' house, when I was small, there were crystals hung on fishing line over the kitchen sink. They were like small ornaments, light-catchers, and when the sun came through the glass in the mornings, the whole kitchen was filled with bright wiggling rainbows of light, and we were mesmerized by the beauty and magic of it. It was so strange and surprising to us that Grandma's tidy house, with vacuumed carpet lines and fine lace doilies, could become such a wild, beautiful place with all those jumping bands of color. It was like having a disco ball in the kitchen, and it made us giggle and bounce with the sheer energy of all that beauty.

That's how it is now, like these small simple things, this tiny child and this blank screen, have turned the living room into a wonderland, bouncing and brimming over unexpectedly with beauty and color and bands of light.

carrying my own weight redux

I owe my body an apology. Technically, I owe my body thousands of apologies, for the thousands of times I've accused it, pushed it, pulled it, starved it, stuffed it, made fun of it, lied about it, hid it, hated it. But now I owe it another one, and I also owe it my gratitude, long overdue, and for the first time, sincere.

I'm sorry for taking you for granted, for wishing you were different, and for abusing you because you looked different than I wanted you to. I'm sorry. And thank you. Thank you for, despite my persecution, being strong and able in the most important way. Thank you for carrying and bearing and nourishing my son.

If bodies lived on love and harmony with the spirits who reside within them, mine would have conked out a long time ago. I fed it a steady diet of hate, venom, and fat-free pseudo food for decades. Someone asked me recently when my poor relationship with my body began. I remember being at Disneyland, wearing little yellow corduroy shorts with a rainbow elastic belt that had a tiny plastic change purse attached to it. I remember being in the bathroom there, in my own stall, and feeling shameful and embarrassed and angry about my legs, and feeling like my yellow shorts were too short. I was six.

Poor girl. Poor body. What this collection of blood and guts has been through makes me weep for it now. If I had known when I was fifteen or twenty what my body would do at thirty, maybe I could have been more gracious with it. Although, come to think of it, I wouldn't have. You could have told me that I was going to give birth to a dozen ten-pound babies when I was thirty, but when I was fifteen, I still would have looked at you in all seriousness and asked, "But what size pants will I be wearing home from the hospital?"

I was always a little nervous about being pregnant. First, there's the general nervousness about being able to get pregnant. We spend all these years taking little pills to not get pregnant, and then many of us find out we didn't need them all along. I felt a serious, deep gratitude when I became pregnant. I was also a little nervous because my mom was very sick when she was pregnant, and because she miscarried more than once, late into the pregnancies. But the gift I was given was an easy pregnancy—a relative term, but I was almost never sick and never in pain.

I was, however, as big as a house, and toward the end, had heartburn so bad that I slept sitting up and kept Tums lined up on the nightstand like little pastel soldiers ready for battle. In the grand scheme of pregnancy, though, a little heartburn certainly pales in comparison to greater complications, and for that I am thankful.

So all of a sudden, this body that I had been mad at for over two decades, this body that had been betraying me over and over, this same body was carrying and creating and nourishing another body. This stubborn collection of bones and flesh became a home, a host for an entirely new person during the most crucial time in his life. I was astonished, and humbled.

As I watched my belly grow, on one hand, I was self-conscious. Being pregnant felt dangerously similar to being fat. It sent me back to shame and regret, feeling like I was out of control, like I was in a car accident and was skidding slowly toward something I had already hit over and over again.

I practiced telling myself the things I told my girlfriends when they were pregnant and self-conscious about being fat. I told myself that to nourish a small person is a sacred thing, and that the power it takes to grow a person is so much more important than how you look in the process. I told myself that pregnancy is beautiful because of what it represents, that it is a symbol of new life and possibility. I told myself all of these things, and while I agreed with them cognitively, it is much easier to believe them now that I am no longer pregnant.

But the only thing harder than being pregnant is being just-no-longer pregnant. Right away, you long to go back to being pregnant, for two reasons. First, because when you were pregnant, at least you had a very good reason to look like Jabba the Hutt, and second, because when you were pregnant, every time your baby needed to eat in the middle of the night, you didn't have to get out of bed.

One of the greatest things right after Henry was born was a hot shower. I think it was one of the only times I felt truly alone. I took very long, very hot showers, with lots of lavender soap, and I just stood there in the steam until the hot water ran out. The one problem with the shower was that it required me to take my clothes off. I don't know who is more glad that this is a book and not a movie, me or you, but just take my word for it: the damage was severe and widespread. I have stretch marks that look like Wolverine tried to dig for buried treasure in my stomach, and it looks like I'm wearing a fanny pack full of pudding under my clothes all the time.

I managed well enough at Christmas parties, with enough strategic undergarments and optical illusions, but there was nowhere to hide on vacation after Christmas. My brother's girlfriend joined us, a darling little person who works out a lot and certainly is not wearing a fanny pack of pudding under her clothes. That didn't help. I'm glad she came, but just between you and me, I kind of wished she were a lot fatter.

I saw a woman at the store, maybe three months after Henry's birth, and she told me that I'm prettier than I used to be, before Henry was born. What a strange, unhelpful thing to say. And I'm certainly not any prettier than I used to be, especially with cavernous black circles under my eyes. But I get what she was saying, somehow. I'm different than I used to be. Different in my skin and my bones, but even more different in my own eyes.

I gained a new respect for my body, for bodies that carry babies, and now when I see pregnant women in my neighborhood or at a store, I think about how strong and powerful those bodies are, how hard they're working. I also think graceful, loving thoughts for those women, knowing that their maternity pants are probably falling down, and that their shoes are probably too tight, and that they probably need a few Tums.

What changed my mind and body, in a very serious way, was the actual experience of birth. What bodies can do in those moments will take your breath away. I am a scared, squeamish person who faints at the sight of blood and threw up during our birthing class and had to watch the rest from the hallway outside the ladies' room door, but if I could relive the experience of Henry's birth every day, I would, absolutely. It felt sacred and overwhelming and full of beauty and prayer. And the fact that this body was able to do that thing silences all those voices that have been yelling at it for years.

This body might not look like much on the outside, and believe me, post-baby, it doesn't. But it did what it came to do on that day, and for that, I am grateful, and for that, I offer it my most sincere apologies.

writing in pencil

I just turned thirty, and I'm finally willing to admit something about life, or at least about my life, and it's this: I should have written in pencil. I should have viewed the trajectory of my life as a mystery or an unknown. I should have planned lightly, hypothetically, and should have used words like "maybe" and "possibly." Instead, every chance I got, I wrote in stone and Sharpie. I stood on my future, on what I knew, on the certainty of what life would hold for me, as though it was rock. What I know now is that instead of rock, it's more like a magic carpet, a slippy-slidy-wiggly thing, full of equal parts play and terror. The ground beneath my feet is lurching and breaking, and making way for an entirely new thing every time I look down, surprised once again by a future I couldn't have predicted.

When I was in high school, I was certain, beyond certain, that I would go to an Ivy League school in New York. I visited in the fall and was totally taken with the turning leaves and majestic buildings, and there was a bell that rang when fresh cookies came out of the oven at the student center. It was magical, and I could see in my mind's eye very clear images of my college self in roll-neck sweaters, wearing

203

a backpack, crossing between gothic buildings with spires and their names carved in stone. I applied early, and the first great disappointment of my life was being rejected from Cornell.

My teachers and college counselors and I analyzed it to death—I should have taken the SAT one more time, my GPA could have been higher, my activity and club lists could have been more focused. I dragged my feet through the rest of the college application process, terrifying my parents, who were afraid I would end up at home with them, driving them crazy. In a last minute decision, one that felt keenly spiritual and distinctly unlike the rest of the process, I chose Westmont, a small college known more for its ocean view than its architecture. It was a wonderful, rich place for me. It was a playground of ideas and words, populated with people who figured heavily into my spiritual development.

In college, I just knew that I would be a professor, that after graduation, I would start a PhD program, maybe in Providence or San Francisco, and would spend my twenties smoking cigarettes and having wild dinner parties in city apartments crammed with books. I would drink red wine and date strange but fabulously intelligent men, many of them foreign, and I would wear vintage shoes and lots of silver jewelry. When I graduated from college, though, I moved back to my hometown outside Chicago. I thought it would be just for a year, while I worked on grad school applications and selected a program. What I found, though, is that I spent far more time with the high school kids I worked with at church than working on my applications or papers. After a year, I bought a house and put the applications away and continued to spend most of my time with the students I worked with, at their games and recitals and retreats and camps.

After Aaron and I were married, I could see our future unfolding, certainly, in our hometown. I had an eye on the neighborhood we'd move into when kids came along, taking into account school district and proximity to grandparents. Our favorite Italian restaurant, Café Clemenza, was about two minutes from our house, and our mall just got an Anthropologie, which seemed like a true sign from above that we should stay put. A year and a half after we were married, we moved to Grand Rapids. Grand Rapids is not known for its Italian food or its shopping, but it is full of smart, passionate, creative people who make our lives feel rich and full of good things.

After I had been working in churches for almost a decade, I assumed that I would continue in that vein for the length of my career. And now I don't. Now I write and play with my baby. I spend about twenty-nine days a month in jammies, at home, writing some and mostly playing with Henry, and then on that odd thirtieth day, I wear heels and lipstick and do work-y things, like meetings or readings.

And the day to day of my life shocks me with its goodness. I sleep well, although not nearly enough, and I feel like my smaller, quieter life fits me just about perfectly for now. To my deep surprise, I don't very often find myself longing to return to the way I lived for so many years.

At a certain point, I have to wonder about my judgment or my sanity. How can I continue knowing so definitively what the future will hold, and then continue being so totally wrong? This is my new thing: I'm going to write in pencil.

Life with God at its core is about giving your life up to something bigger and more powerful. It's about saying at every turn that God knows better than we know, and that his

Spirit will lead us in ways that we couldn't have predicted. I have known that, but I haven't really lived that.

There is a loosey-goosey feeling to the future now, both a slight edge of anxiety, like anything can happen, and a slight bubble of hope and freedom that, well, anything can happen.

There are moments when I feel, suddenly, lucky and thankful and shocked at how happy I am. I have called this the hardest season in my adult life, which it is, and it is not what I had planned in the least, but it is also a secretly beautiful, special season at the same time. It's hard, because some relationships still feel broken, and because we have a lot less money, and because I am afraid, sometimes, about the future, but at the same time, I surprise myself with how okay it is and how okay I am with not knowing exactly what will come next.

I went for a walk a few months ago with my friend Rosa. She's an elder at our church and has four kids. Her husband owns a successful dental practice, and they have a beautiful home where they entertain a lot. The last few years they've been traveling more and more, helping churches all over the world, and have recently decided to move to North Africa with their kids.

As we talked about it, I commented that this season, while they're selling their house and getting ready to move, must feel like an interim season. And she stopped for a second and looked at me pointedly. "You know, Shauna," she said, "everything is interim. Every season that I thought was stable and would be just how it was for a long time ended up being a preparation or a path to the next thing. When you decide to be on this journey with God, everything is interim." When I got back home I wrote that phrase on a Post-It and keep it near my computer.

Everything is interim. Everything is a path or a preparation for the next thing, and we never know what the next thing is. Life is like that, of course, twisty and surprising. But life with God is like that exponentially. We can dig in, make plans, write in stone, pretend we're not listening, but the voice of God has a way of being heard. It seeps in like smoke or vapor even when we've barred the door against any last-minute changes, and it moves us to different countries and different emotional territories and different ways of living. It keeps us moving and dancing and watching, and never lets us drop down into a life set on cruise control or a life ruled by remote control. Life with God is a daring dream, full of flashes and last-minute exits and generally all the things we've said we'll never do. And with the surprises comes great hope.

When it comes right down to it, of course, it's always been in the interim. We've always been in the middle space, the not-yet-heaven middle space, the yearning and groaning. We construct elaborate castles of business cards and Pottery Barn catalogs, and craft armor out of skinny jeans and insurance policies and text messages, beating back the sense that we are not enough, that life is not offering us enough, but we are not and it isn't.

All of life is in the interim, and if we're honest and tender with ourselves, if the armor is off and the castle has crumpled, we feel the ache of the meantime. Our permanent records are a mess of marks and offenses, and we are laid bare to the ache of what's coming.

My dad used to have one of those cars where you can plug in your destination and the woman's voice will tell you where to turn and when to stop to get you there. And when you get there, she says, in this totally dramatic, slightly sexy, slow voice, "You. Have. Arriiiiiived." And we burst out laughing at each other the first time we heard it. We wanted her to say it again. We wanted to plug in more places, and then go to them, just so that she would tell us again that We. Have. Arrived. It was the greatest car in the world. You knew, cognitively, that she was a computer, and that she was only talking about arriving at the dry cleaner, but another part of you just melted when she said it. "Me? Me? I've arrived? Thank you! Say it again!"

That's what I want. I want to arrive. I want to get to wherever I'm going and stay there. That's why I was such a ferocious planner of my life. But I'm learning to just keep moving, keep walking, keep taking teeny tiny steps. And it's in those teeny tiny steps and moments that I become, actually, who I am. We won't arrive. But we can become. And that's the most hopeful thing I can think of.

Thank God I was wrong about everything I had planned. Thank God we weren't on my schedule, because even though I dragged my heels and checked my planner every five seconds while I watched my life change in his hands, I really like the place we've ended up, and the things I've seen along the way. Now when I think about the future, I think about Rosa, and I try to write in pencil.

happy thanksgiving

One snowy night halfway through December, we hosted housechurch at our house, and in a fit of dementia and good intentions, I decided to cook a Thanksgiving dinner. Yes, with a turkey. Yes, even though I barely know how to cook boneless skinless chicken breasts. Yes, even though I have a newborn. Yes, several weeks after the actual holiday.

But it had been ages since we'd hosted housechurch, since before Henry was born, and I missed it, missed the cooking and the table setting and the sounds of their voices in our home, and I wanted it to be special, to feel like a party or a holiday. And I realized as well that I wanted to celebrate the holiday with them. We talk about being one another's family, and that has become so true that when a family time comes, like a holiday, it doesn't feel right to spend it without them.

I had two Thanksgiving dinners already this year, one with my parents and Aaron and Henry. It was the Wednesday before Thanksgiving, actually, which was my mom's birthday. I had watched Rachael Ray make stuffing on her show with caramelized onions and apples, so I tried that, and because there were only a few of us, we did a little turkey breast, instead of the whole deal. The next day, at Aaron's parents' house, we had a fabulous meal. My mother-in-law was planning on cooking, but her back went out, and so one of their friends, a caterer, cooked double and brought over his amazing fancy Thanksgiving food. Diane's a great cook, but we were all a little thankful for her bad back when we tasted the sausage and mushroom stuffing.

All that to say, even though I did the meal part of Thanksgiving twice, I never did the thanks part, the part where you stop and think about the year, and think about what you're thankful for, or what you've been given, or the gratitude you feel toward the people you love and to God for his good gifts.

And so, Thanksgiving at our house, in December. And December in Grand Rapids, as Annette puts it, is like living in a snow globe. There are months and months in the spring of that ugly dirty snow that dogs have peed in and boots have mashed down, but in December, it's that magical movie snow, with swirling huge flakes and thick blankets of snow on rooftops and yellow streetlamp light making everything look dreamy and just as it should be.

I set the table all fancy, with silver chargers and balloon wine glasses and silver candlesticks with long red tapers, and a platter on the coffee table with seven flutes of champagne. We listened to Sufjan Stevens's new Christmas album, which is beautiful and strange, and of course the turkey took like nine hours longer than the recipe said it would, so we had lots of time to drink our champagne and catch up and cuddle with Henry and Spence before their bedtimes.

When the turkey finally decided to be done, after a zillion years, we sat in the twinkly, candlelit dining room and ate stuffing and smashed potatoes and the old-school green bean casserole with the crunchy onions on top. I had flirted briefly with the idea of making updated, sophisticated green beans, like I saw on the Food Network, with mushrooms cooked in wine and onions, but I couldn't make myself do it, because I love the old-time ones with the cream of celery soup so much.

While we ate, we talked about the time we'd spent with our families over the holiday, about the things that change and the things that never do. Joe, who is an expert at not talking about things he doesn't want to talk about, invited us directly and honestly into some of the decisions he's making this year. We stayed at the table for an extra long time, having seconds and listening. We talked about gratitude, and about how there are things that are easy to be thankful for. Henry, for example, is an uncomplicated happiness, as is my family and my marriage and the housechurch.

What I've found this year, though, is a different kind of gratitude. When I left my job, in the swirling pain and confusion of that season, a few people told me that at some point, I would be happy for this, thankful, even. That didn't sit well with me, and it felt even worse than the clichés about closing doors and opening windows. It felt cruel: not only was I supposed to not be sad, I was supposed to be thankful? It felt inauthentic and creepy, and I swore to myself that even if I healed someday, even if the pain abated, even if I was happy again, I would never ever be thankful for this. I would never be like one of those people who's thankful for cancer because of what it taught them, or thankful for the divorce for teaching them to be independent. I would never be thankful for this.

And then, the week of Thanksgiving, I went with my family to the house of some wonderful, generous family friends. The last time I had been there was the day after I left my job. And being there again brought me right back to that place, and showed me, to my surprise, the distance I had traveled in the intervening months. I looked back through my journal, and I stood in the places I remembered standing on that first trip, and I looked out at the ocean at the same times of day, to see the same colors on the same sky, and I realized I am different. And not only different, but better, and not only better, but thankful.

I am thankful, I realized in those moments, thankful for the breaking of things that needed to be broken, that couldn't have been broken any other way, thankful for the severing that allowed me to fall all the way down to the center of my fear and look it in the face, thankful for being set free from something I didn't even know I was enslaved to. There is a quality in my life that I sense now, like a rumbling bass line, or thunder faraway, and the only phrase I can find to capture it is that it is the feeling of having nothing to lose. I have nothing left to lose. Because I was embarrassed and ashamed in such a deep way, and to my surprise, I'm still here. I'm happy in a new way, free in a new way.

I am all the clichés that made me so mad several months ago. I believe in the gift of pain. I believe that loss deepens us. I believe all those things that made me throw a Larry Crabb book against the wall eight months ago. No offense, certainly, to Larry Crabb, who is a wise person, but I was nowhere near ready for his words at the time. I am grateful for God's graciousness toward me that he would teach me these things. And I could gag at that sentence, for how Pollyanna it sounds. As much as I hate to admit it, I've found a new gratitude, and it's gratitude for the way God has redeemed darkness and pain, for the way he brings something beautiful out of something horrible. That's the kind of gratitude we talked about on our snowy Thanksgiving night.

We talked about the ways that God's hand has reached through the darkness in each of our lives. And in those moments, we became more than the sum of our parts, and more than we had been, previously, as a community.

While our babies slept upstairs, and the leftovers and turkey bones littered the table, we told the stories that no one tells, the stories of the darkest places, the most painful moments, and the ways God has held those moments up and turned them from ash to luminous things, treasures, shards of hope.

When we stood in a circle to pray and close our night together, we held hands and thanked God for the darkness, and for the way the darkness had become light, and in that moment, we practiced Thanksgiving. Thanksgiving for the uncomplicated happiness of babies and friendship and food, and for the very complicated joys that come from loss, from failure, from reaching the bottom and pushing back up to the light.

That's a Happy Thanksgiving.

soup from bones

This week I made soup from bones, which is a very practical act of redemption. It's essentially making a meal out of things that would otherwise become garbage, which makes me feel like a pioneer or a war wife, very smart and resourceful. It's amazing to me, really, that it works. Since until very recently, I've never cooked a turkey, I've obviously not acquainted myself with the aftermath, but my mother-in-law made this yummy rich turkey soup last time we were there, and I thought it was worth a try.

I had a college professor that kept a list of things adults must know how to do, and among them is "extemporize a soup." After I learned what "extemporize" meant, I learned to do it with soup, and now it's a word I love to use, because it makes me feel fabulously intelligent, and it makes me think of my professor and of soup. One of the other items on her list was "memorize a passage of Shakespeare," and thanks to her, I can cross that one off, too, although the only passage that remains with me is a laborious passage from a lesser of his plays, chosen, I think, to be ironic and clever. I didn't want to go with the tired "something is rotten in the state of Denmark" or "a rose by any other name," so consequently, all the Shakespeare that's left in my brain is about as pertinent and interesting as directions to a gas station. But I did learn to extemporize, and that's something.

The whole cooking-meat-and-poultry thing is a minor miracle in itself. It's only in the last few years that I've begun experimenting with meat on bones. I feel like we've come so far culturally, you know, with modern medicine and space travel and anti-aging serums, that it feels incongruous to rip flesh from bone with my teeth. It's like rubbing sticks together in the middle of the living room instead of using the lighter in your pocket.

For years, I was a devotee of the twenty-something girl diet of Twizzlers, Ben and Jerry's Cherry Garcia frozen yogurt, and Diet Coke, instead of really fattening things like protein and nutrients. I lived on black coffee and bagels for the better part of a decade. Meats were a foreign concept, like car repair.

Annette knew about my meat-on-the-bone problem, and when I went home from college with her for the weekend, like a good hostess, she told her mom about it. When we sat down for a formal dinner that night, each plate had a roasted, gleaming Cornish game hen, except for my plate, which had a tidy little pile of bite-size pieces of meat, without a bone in sight. I was very appreciative, even though it did look like maybe a three-year-old was joining them for dinner in my place. I should have asked for a sippy cup and a bib.

At a certain point, in the interests of being a grower, I began to tiptoe into the carnivore world. I started with ribs, which might seem like a leap, but to my thinking, at least their bones are all in a row, so there's as little sucking and wrestling as possible. If I'm feeling very courageous, I can manage buffalo wings, but they're so small it almost makes it worse, like I'm a huge giant nibbling on a teeny tiny wing.

I roasted a chicken last year, because Nigella Lawson, whose books I adore, insists that it's so easy and that she roasts two a week. Her cookbook said something British and obtuse, like all I have to do is "shove a lemon in its bottom and salt its lovely skin." She didn't mention all the gross things inside of it, or that it would take a day and a half, or that I would need an anatomy book to know what's what.

Needless to say, roasting a turkey for Thanksgiving was a monumental step, and everything in me, after such an exertion, wanted my husband to dispose of the wreckage immediately and without my involvement. I kept thinking, though, of that yummy soup at my mother-in-law's house, and found myself strangely interested in the idea of these bones becoming useful again.

Some little girls loved Barbies or Cabbage Patch Kids. I loved the *Little House on the Prairie* books. Not the show so much, but the books. I got them for my sixth birthday in a yellow cardboard box set and reread them every year. Making soup from bones seemed to me like something that Ma would do in the winter, while Pa was shoveling the roof, or breaking the icicles from the cows' noses so they didn't freeze.

I consulted my *How to Cook Everything* and took some suggestions, which is as close as I get to following a recipe. I broke down some aromatics—that's the Iron Chef way of saying I chopped garlic, onions, carrots, and celery—and boiled the bones in my big red soup pot. I added some leftover turkey and a handful of rice, and all of a sudden, soup!

And that soup, that plain old turkey soup, made me feel like a miracle worker or a magician, bringing something from nothing. I think there's a particular beauty to that idea for me right now because I've spent so long feeling like a pile of bones, and the idea that these old bones can make something lovely and sustaining moves me.

That's the heart of the story, really, the story of God and people and his hands in the world. All through history, he's making soup from bones, life from death, water from rocks, love from hate.

I like the idea of everything being alive, healthy, brimming with spirit and hope. I wish my life was like that. There are moments of life and beauty, but there are also a lot of bones, skeletons from lives already lived, regrets, broken hearts and promises and relationships. Now on my best days, I take a look at each pile of bones and imagine what it would take to make some soup, to repair and redeem, to make something dead into something full of life and flavor.

Sometimes it takes a phone call, or an apology. Sometimes it takes a new promise, even though I've broken so many in the past. Sometimes telling the truth, sometimes giving up something important, sometimes leaving something long dead. And what you get from that pile of bones is soup—warm, rich, full of life and soul and spirit. You get something beautiful out of the trash, which is the whole point.

basement

I haven't told Annette that I saw her basement. I don't think she wants to know. I didn't mean to see her basement, but I was bringing Henry over, because on Mondays and Wednesdays, Emily watches both our boys at Annette's, and on my way in, I knocked over a stepladder with the carseat, and the stepladder knocked over the broom, which clattered all the way down the basement stairs. Such is life with a carseat. I get caught in at least one doorway every time I take Henry anywhere, poor little guy.

This is the thing about Annette's basement: it looks shockingly, surprisingly like my own. And that makes me feel so much better about myself that I want to lay down on the floor for a while and just breathe in the okayness that floods through me.

I don't know if there are things in your life that are harbors and safe houses for all your shame and secrets, things that you would just die if anyone saw or knew about, but for me, I have two. One is my butt, and the other is my basement. I've spent hundreds of hours and thousands of dollars trying to disguise my butt, trying to make it look a lot more like someone else's butt, or at least camouflage it well enough to fade into the surrounding foliage or cityscape. And my basement is like the holding area for everything that's wrong with my life, all the broken down bits and pieces that I have banished from my upstanding, upstairs life, but still lurk, threatening to expose me, in the basement.

Somewhere in the high-achieving, shiny, Midwestern corner of the world I grew up in, it became very clear to me that we are not supposed to have basements like my basement. It's okay to have some shelving, and some tidy boxes and stacks on the shelves. It's okay to have a not-good-enough-for-the-upstairs couch, and the retired TV, and some weights or a treadmill. It is distinctly not okay to have a basement that is a sprawl of framed and unframed art prints, a fondue set that has fallen out of its box, a slipcover and a mattress pad, thousands of CDs spread all over one corner, cobwebs and wrenches and a wallpaper steamer and a stack of all the stained clothes I meant to soak but never have, and mousetraps and dust bunnies and extra toilet paper and forty-seven half-used paint cans. That's not okay. That's what bad, messy people do, people who are (dare I say it?) *lazy*. I have a lazy person basement, and it bothers me a lot in the middle of the night. I can feel it down there, throbbing with shame, threatening to vomit up the stairs and expose me for what I am, a lazy person with a messy basement.

Martha Beck wrote a fabulous article a few years ago about how our homes affect us and demonstrate our selves back to us. She asked the reader to picture the room you love best in your home, and three words to describe it, and then to picture the room you hate the most, and three words to describe it. She said that the words you choose for the room you love are three things that you would like to be, and the three words for the one you hate are the things you're afraid you really are, and really don't want anyone to know. Clever, that Martha Beck.

My basement is all the things that I don't want you to know, that I want to keep covered and out of your sight. I want you to see my living room and my dining room, my best selves, my most charming and evolved selves. But down there, down in the musty, smelly basement are the parts of me that make me embarrassed and sad. Down there are my easily hurt feelings, my adolescent heartbreaks, my public failures, the times I've tried to tell a joke and no one laughed. Down there are the unrequited loves, the left-out feelings, the times when I heard other girls talking about me in the bathroom, both in high school and at church not that long ago. The basement is where all the hidden parts are.

And I want to keep it hidden, and have kept it hidden quite successfully. Until this year. Until I had a baby. Until people I love wanted to help me, and I realized in a panic-stricken moment that if I allowed them to help me, they would see my basement. They would see my basement, and then they would leave, scared and disapproving, shaking their heads and clucking their tongues, knowing that there was always something off about me, come to think of it. They would talk about me in low tones, saying, "We should have known about someone like her. We should have guessed she'd have one of *those* basements."

My friend Lori, who is smart and thoughtful and has fabulous red hair, came over to watch Henry one night, so that Aaron and I could go out for dinner. She played with him, and watched a movie after he went to bed, and it was only the next morning, when I got up to make coffee, that I realized Lori washed our big sink of grimy dirty dishes, which is practically like washing our feet, in its intimacy and discomfort. Not only did she do our dishes, but she loaded and unloaded our dishwasher.

And now she knows about us. Now she knows that the cabinet under our sink is grody and soggy and has little bits of trash and coffee grounds that missed the garbage can all over it. She knows that the dishwasher is kind of unmoored, and that when you open the door, it lurches down like it's going to fall over onto the floor, and you have to catch it with your foot so that the door doesn't slam against the ground. It's one of those things we said we'd fix right when we moved in, but now is normal to us, and we don't even notice it until someone else loads our dishwasher and almost loses their feet.

The idea that my smart, successful friend Lori has seen the cabinet beneath my sink and has risked her feet on our dishwasher door positively floors me. I'm quite certain she doesn't have cabinets like that. But then again, maybe she does. Maybe we all do, somewhere. Maybe it's not your cabinets or your basement or your butt. But I think it's something, and I think you probably spend a lot of time covering it up and thinking about it in the middle of the night. And I think when you let someone into your life far enough to get a glimpse of it, at first you think you're going to pass out, and that that person is going to ruin your reputation as a good person by blabbering about your butt or your cabinets to everyone you know. But a second after that, I think you're going to realize that that person is your friend. Like really and truly, from Jesus, your friend.

That's why Annette's basement healed me so deeply. Because she's one of the other kind of people. There's people like me, and then there's people like her. I have this sense that she's the good, upstanding kind of person, and I, certainly, am not. She wears pretty makeup, and necklaces and cute shoes, and I lurch around in my yoga pants and a ratty ponytail for days on end. She reapplies lipstick throughout the day, and has dress coats and china. She's strong and direct and knows how to do spreadsheets and started her own business, and I can barely email, and if we're being honest, don't understand even the first thing about, say, taxes, or what "net" and "gross" mean.

Her basement doesn't bother me one bit. It's messy and dirty and you have to wind your way through it like a corn maze, and it doesn't even put a dent in how much I love her and respect her and think she's smart. And apparently, against all odds, that's how Lori feels about me, even though she's dealt with my dishwasher. That makes me feel both honest, like she's seen the very worst and there's nothing else to be exposed; and safe, like she's not going to leave or make fun of me. When you find those things coexisting peacefully in one friendship, I think you've got a good thing going there, and you should let them see your basement.

needle and thread

When Henry was born, we brought music into the delivery room that we thought would be the right sounds for him and for me, to serve as the soundtrack for his birth. We played songs by Ben Folds and Snow Patrol and Johnny Cash and the Beatles. Even now, when I listen to that playlist, it takes me back to that room, to the bright light in an otherwise dark room, to the tears running down my mom's face, and to Aaron's wide eyes, looking at once scared and amazed.

Just after Henry was born, and I mean *just* after— when Linda, the nurse, was weighing and measuring him, and his thin little gasping first cries sounded like the most beautiful sounds we had ever heard—at that moment, the only other thing we could hear, in the middle of the night in a silent hospital, was a song called "Needle and Thread" by Sleeping at Last. It's about God and angels and hospitals and love, and in that moment, it became ours—our song, Henry's song. Henry yelped and wiggled under the yellow light of the bassinet, and I laid in the bed motionless, spent and relieved and overwhelmed. I felt emptied in the best possible way, like I had done something brave and portentous, and now my work was done.

We heard the song again a few days later in our car when we brought Henry home from the hospital. Aaron was driving, and I was sitting in the backseat next to Henry in his carseat, my arms stretched over him, shielding him from any possible harm. I was also practicing Jedi mind tricks, willing all the other cars on the road to slow down and back away from our car. I imagined that everyone else on the road was either a bank robber in a getaway car, or a crazy person, or a drunk, and I glared at each one of them, preemptively rage-filled at their recklessness. And then that song began, and my rage and anxiety braided themselves into tense, muscular love. I cried all the way home, thinking about how God and his angels knitted this boy, our boy, together with needle and thread. And I thanked God for that song, and for creating a person who could write that song, our song.

I know that the song isn't about Henry. I don't think it's about birth at all. Maybe it's about someone's uncle, or an episode of *Grey's Anatomy*. It doesn't matter, because the thing about a truly great song is that it becomes, truly and deeply, about our very own lives, regardless of what it started out as when it was written.

A few months later, Aaron and I went to a Sleeping at Last show, and when they played that song, we held hands, and I cried some more, and thought about our boy, about the night he was born, and the ride home, and the thousand moments in between—of life with Henry, and the rich and miraculous thing that it is to be his mother.

I wanted to tell the songwriter about it, about how thankful we were for his song, about how deeply his song traveled through the tenderest parts of our life, about how those words and sounds had become part of the story of one of the most sacred events of our lives. As I walked out to my car after the show, I almost went back to wait in line and tell him, but I knew that I would cry, not sweet little tears, but the kind that make your nose and eyeliner run, and that very possibly I would try to hug him, which would be mortifying for both of us. I don't know a lot about being a rock star, but I do know that just about the last thing a rock star wants, when there is a line of cute twenty-year-old girls in skinny jeans and black nail polish, is a thirty-year-old mom showing him pictures of her baby on her phone, trying to tell him something very personal and weepy about her son.

And so I didn't tell him, but if I had, this is what I would have said: Thank you. Thank you, and keep going. Please keep writing songs. Please keep believing in music, because we do, and we need it, and specifically, we need yours. We need the sounds and words and rhythms of hope and longing and beauty. We need the drums and the strings and the haunting twist of your voice. We need the poetry of your lyrics and the spirit and force of your sounds. We're desperate for great music, and there's so much out there, but never, ever enough. We're desperate for great storytellers, great painters, great dancers, great cooks, because art does something nothing else does.

Art slips past our brains straight into our bellies. It weaves itself into our thoughts and feelings and the open spaces in our souls, and it allows us to live more and say more and feel more. Great art says the things we wished someone would say out loud, the things we wish we could say out loud. When Ryan from Sleeping at Last sings, that's how I would sing, except that I sound like a five-year-old with a head cold when I sing, so I'm so glad that he does the singing, and I do the listening. My friend Anne dances the way I would dance if I could. My friend Sarah creates paintings that make me feel alive and free and like the world is more beautiful than it was before I saw that very painting, and I'm so glad she does, because I sure can't, and because I'm better for having seen her paintings.

It matters, art does, so deeply. It's one of the noblest things, because it can make us better, and one of the scariest things, because it comes from such a deep place inside of us. There's nothing scarier than that moment when you sing the song for the very first time, for your roommate or your wife, or when you let someone see the painting, and there are a few very long silent moments when they haven't yet said what they think of it, and in those few moments, time stops and you quit painting, you quit singing forever, in your head, because it's so fearful and vulnerable, and then someone says, essentially, thank you and keep going, and your breath releases, and you take back everything you said in your head about never painting again, about never singing again, and at least for that moment, you feel like you did what you came to do, in a cosmic, very big sense.

I know that life is busy and hard, and that there's crushing pressure to just settle down and get a real job and khaki pants and a haircut. But don't. Please don't. Please keep believing that life can be better, brighter, broader, because of the art that you make. Please keep demonstrating the courage that it takes to swim upstream in a world that prefers putting away for retirement to putting pen to paper, that chooses practicality over poetry, that values you more for going to the gym than going to the deepest places in your soul. Please keep making art for people like me, people who need the magic and imagination and honesty of great art to make the day-to-day world a little more bearable.

And if, for whatever reason, you've stopped— stopped believing in your voice, stopped fighting to find the time—start today. I bought a mug for my friend, from the Paper Source in Chicago (which is, by the way, a fabulous playground for creative people), and the mug says, "Do something creative every day." Do that. Do something creative every day, even if you work in a cubicle, even if you have a newborn, even if someone told you a long time ago that you're not an artist, or you can't sing, or you have nothing to say. Those people are bad people, and liars, and we hope they develop adult-onset acne really bad. Everyone has something to say. Everyone. Because everyone, every person was made by God, in the image of God. If he is a creator, and in fact he is, then we are creators, and no one, not a bad seventh-grade English teacher or a harsh critic or jealous competitor, can take that away from you.

My friend, Steve, leads a junior-high ministry, and it's a fun, funny, creative group of kids and leaders who get together on Tuesday nights to talk about how to live great lives and make the world better in God's name. He asked me to come one Tuesday night so that he could interview me and let some of the students ask questions. We talked about being a writer and what that's like, and about Henry, and about bands that I like, and after it was over, one girl came up to talk to me. She looked nervous, and a little shy.

"I write, too." She said it like it was a confession or a secret. She leaned toward me and opened a notebook and showed me page after page after page of precise cursive. "Do you have any advice for me?" she asked.

"Thank you, and keep going," I said. "Thank you for writing, for taking the time and spirit and soul to write, because I *love* to read, and I'm so thankful to writers like you, for writing things for me to read. And keep going, even when people make you feel like it's not that important. It might be the most important thing you do. Keep going."

So to all the secret writers, late-night painters, would-be singers, lapsed and scared artists of every stripe, dig out your paintbrush, or your flute, or your dancing shoes. Pull out your camera or your computer or your pottery wheel. Today, tonight, after the kids are in bed or when your homework is done, or instead of one more video game or magazine, create something, anything.

Pick up a needle and thread, and stitch together something particular and honest and beautiful, because we need it. I need it.

Thank you, and keep going.

cold tangerines

I believe in a life of celebration. I believe that the world we wake up to every day is filled to the brim with deep, aching love, and also with hatred and sadness. And I know which one of those I want to win in the end. I want to celebrate in the face of despair, dance when all we see on the horizon is doom. I know that Death knocks at our doors and comes far too early for far too many of us, but when he comes for me, I want to be full-tilt, wide-open, caught in the very act of life. I think that's what we're here for, not for a passive, peaceful life, but to stand up in the face of all that lacks peace and demand more.

If I gave you a sweater, and you loved it, I would know because you would wear it so much you'd be on the verge of wearing it out, because you loved it that much. It would be the sweater you wear on Christmas and to get coffee and that you sleep in sometimes and that you drag around in the back of your car and tie around your waist. It would start to smell like you, and it would get snags and get all stretched out, and just looking at it would make you tell a thousand stories of where it's been and who you've been in it.

That's what I want my life to be, like a well-loved gift.
I think life, just life, just breathing in and out, is a great gift.
God gives us something amazing when he gives us life, and I
want to live with gratitude. I want to live in a way that shows
how much I appreciate the gift. If life were a sweater, I would
wear it every day. I wouldn't save it or keep it for a special
occasion. I would find every opportunity to wear that sweater,
and I'd wear it proudly, shamelessly, for days on end.

There's normal life, kind of day-to-day, make-breakfast,
do-the-dishes kind of life, but just underneath that, like a
throb of bass you feel in your chest, I feel a whole other thing
going on. In the midst of taxes and email, there is something
sacred, something special dipping and weaving within that
same old thing, like a firefly, like a great song, and it reminds
you that the dishes and the taxes are real, but so much more
is real, too. The sacred mixes in with the daily when you have
a conversation with someone you love, or when you read a
great book, or when you do something courageous. It's still
just a normal day, but there's something bigger, something
more compelling going on, too.

One look at a baby's fingers and you just know that
those little bundles of flesh and tiny bones are more sacred,
more spiritual, than any thought or idea or theology could
ever be. There are glimpses and whispers of the divine all
through the daily, if we let ourselves look again, if we let
ourselves believe that the world all around us is threaded
through with divinity.

I live according to my faith when I love a meal that
has been prepared carefully, when I notice texture and color
and taste, when I let the flavor and scent of something fresh
from the ground surprise me and bring me back to life. I
demonstrate my theology when I dance all night with people
I love, because this life is worth the best celebration we can

offer up to it. I thank God every time I eat crusty bread and garlicky olives, and when I smell clean laundry and hear that little squeak of fingers on a guitar. For me, what God said when he made the world is a prayer: It is good. This world, it is good. The beauty of a perfect green apple is good. The first steps of a child are good. Watching my grandparents dance in their kitchen is good. It is good.

I have to remind myself that it is good. I have to create hope in my life, because there's something inside me that has radar for the bad parts of life. I walk into the kitchen and all I can see are crumbs on the counter, and I look in the mirror and don't even see my face, I just see all the potential wrinkles forming. I have a dark, worst-case scenario sensor, and it takes over. It's all true. There are crumbs on the counter. I am definitely getting wrinkles. I just don't want to live in only that reality.

Because there is another reality. A better one. Hope and redemption and change are real, and they're happening all around me. So I choose to act out of that reality, because the other one makes life too hard, day after day. Life is painful, and we carry with us so much disappointment and heartbreak. But I'm fighting to save some space inside me where I can create hope. I can't live there in the disappointment anymore. I've missed whole seasons of my life. I look back and all I remember is pain. I guess I went to work or to class during that time, but I don't really remember. I wasted a lot of time wishing I was different. I didn't love the gift of life because I was too busy being angry about the life I was given. I wanted it to be different. But being angry didn't change those things. It just wasted time. I can't take away the things that have happened to you or to me, but what we have, maybe as a reward for getting through all the other days, is today. Today is a gift. And if we have tomorrow, tomorrow will be a gift.

It's rebellious, in a way, to choose joy, to choose to dance, to choose to love your life. It's much easier and much more common to be miserable. But I choose to do what I can do to create hope, to celebrate life, and the act of celebrating connects me back to that life I love. We could just live our normal, day-to-day lives, saving all the good living up for someday, but I think today, just plain today, is worth it. I think it's our job, each of us, to live each day like it's a special occasion, because we've been given a gift. We get to live in this beautiful world. When I live purposefully and well, when I dance instead of sitting it out, when I let myself laugh hard, when I wear my favorite shoes on a regular Tuesday, that regular Tuesday is better.

Right now, around our house, all the leaves are falling, and there's no reason that they have to turn electric bright red before they fall, but they do, and I want to live like that. I want to say, "What can I do today that brings more beauty, more energy, more hope?" Because it seems like that's what God is saying to us, over and over. "What can I do today to remind you again how good this life is? You think the color of the sky is good now, wait till sunset. You think oranges are good? Try a tangerine." He's a crazy delightful mad scientist and keeps coming back from the lab with great, unbelievable new things, and it's a gift. It's a gift to be a part of it.

I want a life that sizzles and pops and makes me laugh out loud. And I don't want to get to the end, or to tomorrow, even, and realize that my life is a collection of meetings and pop cans and errands and receipts and dirty dishes. I want to eat cold tangerines and sing loud in the car with the windows open and wear pink shoes and stay up all night laughing and paint my walls the exact color of the sky right now. I want to sleep hard on clean white sheets and throw parties and eat ripe tomatoes and read books so good they make me jump up and down and I want my everyday to make God belly laugh, glad that he gave life to someone who loves the gift, who will use it up and wring it out and drag it around like a favorite sweater.

What if, all at once, all the shabby, tired, used-up bodies and minds start to wriggle and pop, like they've been dropped into a deep-fryer, sizzling and dancing, transformed into motion? And something that has been deadened and distracted by the tension and noise of this world comes to life anew, wakes up and wiggles like a fritter in a frying pan, anointed, and taught to dance. Because we were made for motion, for arching up toward God with all the energy and passion of a thunderstorm, lightning slicing through a sleepy world to remind us that we serve a fast-dancing God, a God who set this world whirling and crashing through space so that we could live from our toes and drum out the pulse of a billion veins carrying lifeblood to a billion hearts, temples to a God that got his hands dirty making us from dust. Let's get dirty, in his name. Let's sizzle and pop in his name. Let's dance and shimmer and scrawl out our stories across the sky, like he taught us to. Let's echo his words, and let our lives speak those words: It is good.

acknowledgments

Many thanks to the Willow Creek and Mars Hill communities. A church is a family, and you have both been wonderful, loving families to Aaron, Henry, and me. Dale Griffith at Barrington High School, Diane Cooper and Matt Houston at Kanakuk Kamp, Heather Speirs at Westmont College, and Nancy Ortberg and Rex and Andrea Minor at Willow Creek have been mentors and guides through some of the most crucial passages, and for that I am grateful. You have given me something to aspire to.

Angela Scheff and Becky Shingledecker began as colleagues and have become friends. Many thanks to you both, and thanks also to Chris Ferebee, Scott Heagle, and the very fine people at Zondervan, for your hard work and for your friendship. Many dear friends read draft upon draft of these chapters: loads of thanks to Ruth Olsson, Troy Hatfield, Lori Strehler, Tom Rinks, my parents, Aaron, and the HC. Your words and advice and challenge and support kept me company on the loneliest and wildest days, and the hours you put in, at Kava and at the lake and after the kids were in bed, pen in hand, made these stories better stories.

Without Henry's Aunties Amy and Emily, and without his incomparable Grandmas Diane and Lynne, this book would still be a handful of green Post-Its scribbled between night feedings. Henry and I both thank you. What a lucky boy he is to be loved so well by each one of you.

Books and their authors have been my guides, my prophets, and my friends. I have learned from, lived by, and carried with me the stories and phrases of books that I've loved. To the writers who have shaped me, shared their stories with me, wept with me, and rejoiced with me through the pages of their books, may this serve as one more tiny burst of light in a glittering night sky.

To connect with Shauna
and to check out new stories and upcoming events,
please go to shaunaniequist.com.

Share Your Thoughts

With the Author: Your comments will be forwarded to the author when you send them to *zauthor@zondervan.com*.

With Zondervan: Submit your review of this book by writing to *zreview@zondervan.com*.

Free Online Resources at
www.zondervan.com/hello

 Zondervan AuthorTracker: Be notified whenever your favorite authors publish new books, go on tour, or post an update about what's happening in their lives.

 Daily Bible Verses and Devotions: Enrich your life with daily Bible verses or devotions that help you start every morning focused on God.

 Free Email Publications: Sign up for newsletters on fiction, Christian living, church ministry, parenting, and more.

 Zondervan Bible Search: Find and compare Bible passages in a variety of translations at www.zondervanbiblesearch.com.

 Other Benefits: Register yourself to receive online benefits like coupons and special offers, or to participate in research.